Cindy —

This book was written by our special friend — Chef Jani of Finland. His passion for cooking and zest for life makes each meal with him a true dining experience. We hope you enjoy this cookbook and try some of the awesome recipes included here.

Merry Christmas 2010,

Don & Ann Vardeman

bright sky press
HOUSTON, TEXAS

2365 Rice Boulevard, Suite 202,
Houston, Texas 77005
www.brightskypress.com

10 9 8 7 6 5 4 3 2 1

Energy cuisine : two chefs, four countries, one extraordinary friendship / David Denis and Jani Lehtinen.
p. cm.
ISBN 978-1-933979-97-7 (hardcover)
1. Denis, David, 1970- 2. Lehtinen, Jani, 1972- 3. Cooks—Texas—Houston. 4. Cooks—Finland—Pori.
5. Cooking—Miscellanea. I. Lehtinen, Jani, 1972-

TX649.A1E54 2010
641.5—dc22   2010031681

Creative Direction by Ellen Cregan
Design by Wyn Bomar; Photography by Shannon O'Hara
Printed in China through Asia Pacific Offset

energy cuisine

TWO CHEFS. FOUR COUNTRIES.
One Extraordinary Friendship.

David Denis and Jani Lehtinen
with John DeMers
Photography by Shannon O'Hara

energy*cuisine*

CONTENTS

When I met David Denis and Jani Lehtinen, seven years apart but in the same restaurant, it was their energy that impressed me the most. Both are chefs who own restaurants, which invariably means long hours and doing every job in the house at one time or another. And both could look back on long years of training and apprenticeship, in Europe a kind of barely dignified slavery that never entirely ceases to leave its mark. Both chefs could cook up a storm, it became clear: David, the cuisine of his native South of France and Jani, the cuisine of Italy he had discovered away from his native Finland, thanks to a beloved aunt's marriage. I could tell that here were stories waiting to be told, stories of work and family and love, stories driven by food and wine. Here were stories I felt compelled to read, so I simply had to help write them first.

Still, the fascinating friendship this book chronicles, and indeed the title of this book, never would have happened without a quirky twist of business fate. The city in which David operates his business (Houston, Texas) and the city in which Jani operates his (Pori, Finland) both feature what have come to be known as Energy Corridors. These are areas built up around the global energy industry, the big oil and gas companies for starters, but also the hundreds and hundreds of smaller companies that supply their every need. Intriguingly, both David and Jani found success in the restaurant business by earning the trust and admiration of executives within their respective Energy Corridors.

It was precisely those executives, traveling back and forth between Texas and Finland, who decided that Jani had to eat in David's Houston restaurant, Le Mistral. And it was Jani who tasted the food there and decided he had to meet the chef. To say that the rest is history is merely a beginning. Since David and Jani hit it off immediately, the rest is also hijinks, eating and drinking, laughter and innumerable transatlantic trips to cook in each other's restaurants. Regular diners in both places look forward to these two-chefs-for-the-price-of-one evenings, with reservations for the private rooms and chef's tables at a premium.

All of us involved in this book project agreed that several things had to be included. Each chef had to tell his life story, for instance. The effect, it turned out, was almost novelistic, with childhoods lived so far apart, training in entirely different culinary traditions, and businesses launched on far sides of an ocean, yet many deep beliefs about the nature of food, wine and, most of all, life held in common. If this was to be a "buddy picture," it was one in which most of the plot was less shared than parallel.

Of course, there had to be recipes, what we all came to refer to as "yours, mine and ours." Each restaurant has its signatures dishes, naturally, so diners would appreciate (all right, demand) that at least some of their favorites follow them home at the end of the night. But there were also many recipes, of which we've chosen the best to share with you, that David and Jani came up with together. In recent years, they haven't been visiting each other's restaurants just for their health, you know; they've been collaborating on menus for special clients that have traveled the world (the menus, not just the clients!) even more than they have.

And finally, there was The Adventure. That's what we called it anyway, and indeed that's what it became. David and Jani insisted, despite all logic and all budgetary good sense, that photographer Shannon O'Hara and I not only produce this book with them but travel with them to all the places that really mattered. That meant Jani's Finland in late winter (which in turn meant buying heavier clothes), and it meant David's South of France in early spring. They insisted we see and chronicle where their inspiration comes from, where their best ingredients come from and, yes, where they come from, as though the answer to the puzzle that lies within each of us can be found in the place we began.

Having celebrated The Adventure with David, Jani and Shannon, and having toasted our oh-so-profound insight with more than a little wine, I can't promise you that we're all and only where we came from. But I can promise you I now believe it about two chefs with enough energy to power their own Energy Corridors.

Since David and Jani hit it off immediately, the rest is also hijinks, eating and drinking, laughter and innumerable transatlantic trips to cook in each other's restaurants.

My relationship with the restaurant business, you might say, began many years before I was born. My grandmother operated a *routier* in the South of France, one of those simple places that used to turn up along the routes— the highways, if you prefer. If you were being kind, you might translate *routier* to mean "cafe," except that in France that word means something different, something a few steps up the pecking order. No, the best way to translate *routier* into English is "truck stop," and certainly a big part of my Meme's clientele were the men who drove huge, rumbling loads past her

front door day and night, connecting every corner of France with dry goods, meats and seafood, fresh produce and flowers. Another part of her customer base was made up of lonely traveling salesmen, who would often get a small room in town for the night and need somebody to fix them a good dinner. My Grandma, for many years, was that somebody.

I say all this right at the beginning because I'm pretty sure what you're thinking about French cuisine. I heard it time and again when I first started cooking for Americans in Europe and, later, when I came to America to pursue my dream. French food, I'd be told, is always fancy, always expensive and always served with a really bad attitude. Snobbish. Superior. Snooty. There are, naturally, in France and around the world, a few French restaurants that enjoy the luxury of being and acting that way. But not many. And they are as foreign to me, even after all these years, as they are to you.

The typical Frenchman's idea of food is humble, fresh, flavorful and simple, the kind of thing we've now learned to call "comfort food." And in France, as in America, the very best comfort foods are those that remind us of the best things we tasted growing up. The best things we remember eating with our parents. The best things that, day after day, my grandmother served at her truck stop. I hope you think about that the next time you imagine me as one of those obnoxious French chefs you see in the movies. I have absolutely worked for a few guys like that, and believe me, you can't possibly hate them half as much as I do.

Two women—my Meme and my mother—played a large part in teaching me my approach to French food. A larger part, in fact, than any single French chef. By the time I entered this world, Meme had essentially "moved up," running a brasserie in the town of La Seyne. And for much of my childhood, my mother ran a restaurant in Le Revest les Eaux. If this job didn't require toughness enough on my mother's part, I now understand better that her toughest job was bringing up me and my brother, Sylvain, after my father died when I was only 13. That would have made Sylvain 6 at the time, and it must have been incredibly difficult for her, spending those two last years caring for my father and then taking over the care and feeding of, well, us. I think of the qualities all of that required from my mother: tireless labor, patience, strength and honesty. I'd like to think that, in some small way, those values rubbed off on Sylvain and me. There's certainly not a day that I don't hope they did.

My dad's final years also played a role in my career decision, since my mother had so much to deal with that she often sent me off to stay with Meme. This meant cooking together, at home or at her brasserie. After a hard day, she and I would sit and eat our dinner together (cooks eat last, all over the world) and talk. That lady had so many stories—about different rustic foods and the people who grew the ingredients she used, about her staff (in a restaurant, always the source of much local color) and of course about the strange, unintentional comedy act put on daily by her customers. I loved her stories; little by little, I decided I loved her life. By the time I was 16, with our family's financial difficulties, I knew I had to go out and make money. I wanted to do that, I now knew, by working in the kitchen.

Over the next six or seven years, I combined the very traditional European chef apprenticeship with the newer addition of culinary schooling. I understood, in some juvenile way, the challenges ahead, and I knew I had to be good. Several times when others in my group peeled away to work and earn money, I kept at my studies. I wasn't sure what I had to be good enough for. I only knew I had to be ready for anything. Yes, you might say, I was obsessed. Or possessed. You Americans might also say that it was a good look for me!

There were three years studying cooking at the Ecole de Beausset in Beausset, my earliest training alternating two weeks in the classroom with two weeks in various professional kitchens. In the classroom, I was

hopeless: I was too hyper, couldn't sit still and five hours felt like forever. But in the kitchen, where every minute was utterly different from the one before, I could work for 15 hours straight, go home and show up early the next day. Even at that age, 17 or 18, I understood the great truth that when your job is doing something you love, something that's your passion, it doesn't feel like a job at all.

This continued through advanced training (sort of like a master's degree in cooking) at a different culinary school near Paris, in the town of Blois. And man, that was a hard life. I had no money (not for the first or, as it turned out much later in America, the last time), and six of us cooks slept in bunk beds in one room with one shower. Even that shower was one too many in the icy winter, since the chef who owned the place was too cheap to turn on the heat. That man was definitely a screamer of what I call the "barbarian style," and he was a big thrower as well. When he got mad, he'd throw his rock-hard chef clogs at our faces, and whether they hit the target or not, the "guilty party" had to retrieve them with head hanging low and carry them back to the chef.

I got out of that place as soon as I'd finished my studies and, since my mother was struggling as a single mom with Sylvain, I knew it was all about the paycheck. I signed on at the famous Hotel le Carlton in Cannes (yes, where the movie stars converge once a year for that film festival), where I impressed my bosses enough to make me their youngest saucier ever. I was really proud of that. And then, to gain some head-chef experience, I moved from big to small, taking over a four-person kitchen at the Restaurant le Bois de Lune-Montvenix in Savoie in the French Alps. My learning continued for three years in Switzerland, at the Hotel le Gashof Baren in Aarau, about 40 minutes from Zurich. By then I'd been cooking, with classroom and without, for more than a decade. I didn't know it yet, and it happened in several stages, but Texas was about to walk into my life and change the course of it forever.

An extremely wealthy American family, who spent their summers on the French Riviera, had just fired their private chef, the guy who did all the shopping, cooked all the meals and staged all the many parties, indoors and out. I heard about the job from a friend, and also that this family was looking for a woman chef. All jokes about showing up in drag aside, I thought maybe I could convince them to hire me for that summer. I got an interview time, showed up and waited for about five hours for the lady of the house to see me, all the while being handed glass after glass of red wine. We talked, as best I could still talk, and she told me what she was looking for. And I told her that I couldn't be a woman but, as a chef with summers off from my hotel in Switzerland, I would be an excellent choice. She must have agreed.

I spent the next five years of my life as personal chef to this wealthy American family, initially only on the Riviera during the summers, and then more and more being called in to cook a week here or there at their many houses around the world. Eventually, even my "day job" in Switzerland seemed to get in the way, so I left and worked entirely for different branches of this family. It got funny sometimes, though, with family members squabbling over who could have me where for this weekend, in this or that state, this or that country. I had to choose, and after a lot of thinking, I decided to work full time for the daughter of the woman who'd first interviewed me. Through all those years of cooking and traveling by private jet and helicopter (and yes, being paid more to do less than I'd ever been in my life), the city called Houston, Texas, came to feel more and more like home.

When I first went to America, I remember, my uncle took me aside and said, "I don't think you'll ever come back to France." And I asked him, with disbelief and maybe some anger, "What the hell are you talking about?" After several years, I came to understand that he'd been right.

To be honest with you, I started to feel guilty. Mine was such an easy life. I know, it sounds weird. It might even sound crazy. But after all my training and all that abuse by the kinds of French chefs I now try never to be, and most of all, after the hard-working, honest example of my mother, I just couldn't do it anymore. I needed to feel better about my work each day. I needed to feel true to myself. And surrounded by my own new example—Houston—I understood that the best way to be true to myself was to own my own business. To become the kind of entrepreneur I saw passing through all those mansions I was always cooking in. Win or lose, I'd then know that my fate was my own.

Well, OK. Not entirely my own. By this point my "fate" included my young American wife, Elena, and the children we were hoping we'd have. I was playing tennis on a Sunday morning when I first saw her, carrying two huge baskets of laundry toward the washers in the apartment

complex where we both lived. I must have liked what I saw, for I halted my tennis game and helped her with those baskets. It was a super-hot, super-humid summer day in Houston, and when the tennis game had ended, she met me by the court with an ice-cold drink. We were seldom apart from that day for-ward, and after several years of dating (you know, the way we Frenchmen like to do!), Elena encouraged me to see the error of my French ways and actually get married like a good, solid American.

Opening the first Le Mistral was a tough but unforgettable experience. First, I made a phone call home to France and encouraged Sylvain to abandon his architecture career (for at least two years, I told him) to help me, running the front of the house and becoming my expert on wines. And then we had to find a location to lease, which we did basically out in the woods in West Houston, on some thoroughfare with cows on it named Eldridge Parkway. We found a place in a strip center that a guy was trying to get out of, leased it and went to work. Because we had no money once all the savings from my private chef days were gone, Sylvain and I did everything we could ourselves. Elena helped too. And even her father, a very successful Texas attorney, could be spotted painting the walls in the restaurant's bathrooms.

So...we pick our opening day. It was to be September 14, in the year 2001. Unfortunately, September 11 came first.

As you may remember, the nation's restaurant business ground to a halt after the terrorist attacks on 9/11, and that meant that our business ground to a halt before it even opened. Sylvain and I survived mostly because we worked in a restaurant, where there was always some cheap pasta to cook. And we survived again a couple years later, when the United States and France had a falling-out over the Iraq War. You know, "freedom fries" and all that. Television images of Americans pouring French wines down the drain. As the guy who had to pay for those wines to serve in my restaurant, that certainly broke my heart. But my customers stuck with us till that had passed. Some of them even asked me how I felt about it. I told them, "Look, I'm just a chef. I don't have anything to do with all that."

We worked hard, we worked long and we worked for practically no money. But our business grew, year after year. And wonder of wonders, after a while, there weren't any cows on Eldridge Parkway anymore. They were replaced by huge steel and glass office buildings housing the major oil companies, along with the hundreds of other companies from all over the world that support them. Eldridge started to go by a different name: the Energy Corridor. And the people who grew their careers up and down that Energy Corridor became some of my best customers. They are to this day.

After seven years in that strip center, Sylvain and I decided it was time to dream again. And this being America, that dream didn't include leasing anything from anybody. I like to joke that seven years of hard work let us move a whole 150 feet! We managed to buy an acre of land next to the original Le Mistral and build an 11,000-square-foot restaurant complex, with a dining room seating 70 people, an upstairs banquet room seating 80, a very European courtyard for receptions and even a space we've now turned into a French bakery and gourmet shop. Best of all, we put in a large (I'd had it with all those tiny kitchens) glistening European-style cooking space, which, instead of the typical American line facing the wall, allows chefs and cooks to work around an "island" facing each other. Somehow people just don't understand how much communication is required to fix the perfect lunch or dinner for you. This is the new Le Mistral.

Today, I have the pleasure of working with my own brother in a restaurant that features many of our mother's paintings of the Provençal countryside on the walls. I have the pleasure of being an American-style success for my wife, Elena (who's a psychotherapist, which makes her perfect to be married to a French chef), and for our two children, Emilie and Luc (who I'm hoping will grow up speaking French as well as English in this strange place called Houston, Texas). Having dreamed a big dream a few times in my life, I have the pleasure of seeing it come true. And I don't just live my dream each and every day. Thanks to America, I now know its street address.

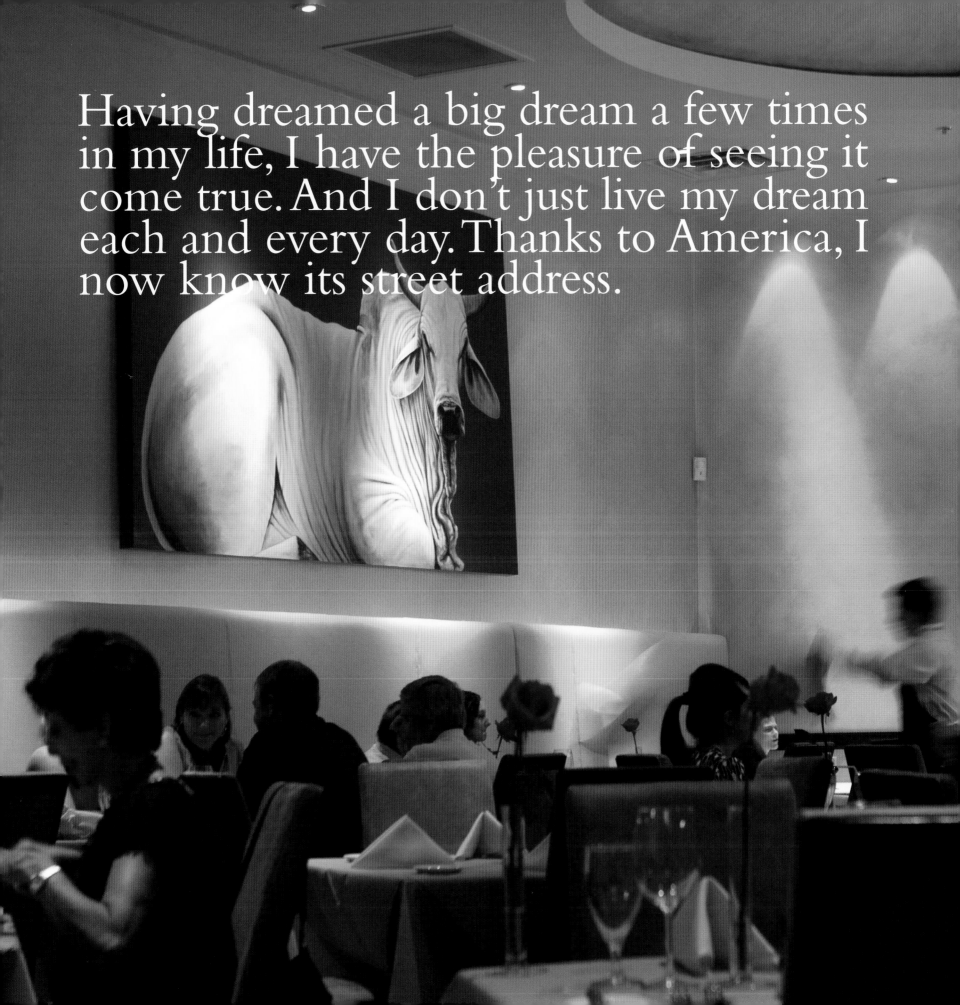

Having dreamed a big dream a few times in my life, I have the pleasure of seeing it come true. And I don't just live my dream each and every day. Thanks to America, I now know its street address.

I bet you've met a lot of Italian chefs, and I bet they're all named something like Carlo or Luigi or Antonio. These days, you'll even meet the occasional Italian chef named Maria or Tomasina. But I'm guessing you've never met one named Jani, one who pronounces his first name "Yani," no less. In fact, you may never have met an Italian chef who owns and cooks in a restaurant called Bucco, serving mostly Italian dishes in Pori, a city of

80,000 people on the seaside about 240 kilometers northwest of Helsinki. Yes, you're absolutely right. That would be in Finland.

The story of how I came to be an "Italian chef" in my native, very northern land is both very complicated and very simple. It was inspired by the simple act of my aunt marrying someone from Italy and going there to live. But it was also born of my own deep recognition, when I went to visit her for a summer when I was 17 and then many more times over the years, that here on the Italian table was food I understood. Strange? Yes, maybe. But in food terms, it was nothing more than an experience many of us have had, visiting a faraway place for the very first time and feeling as though we've finally come home. For lots of people around the world, even those whose names don't end in vowels, discovering the flavors of Italian food is exactly like that, like coming home.

My menu at Bucco includes items that aren't Italian—some French of course (especially French techniques, as my friend David would make me admit) and also Russian dishes, Scandinavian classics and a few Spanish touches from my recent visits to Spain. But I believe that my early encounters with Italian cuisine taught me everything I really needed to know about what it means to cook. Italians have an innate love of feeding people, of making people happy by feeding them. I swear, *mangia* must be the most popular command in the entire Italian language. But unlike in fancy French restaurants (NO, I don't mean David's wonderful, comfortable Le Mistral), Italian food remains pretty simple, amazingly basic, even at the fanciest levels. Let's face it: most great Italian dishes are made with relatively few ingredients, and usually none that would strike Italian cooks as exotic, as well as surprisingly few difficult procedures. Most Italian food is what I like to call Mama Food, or even Grandma Food, and you can't say anything better than that about food in any language.

I spent my childhood in Pori; it was a traditional childhood in the sense that both my parents were born there. I did the things that all children around Pori do growing up, like crunching on raw local vegetables the minute they came into their season. As you can guess, when they went out of season, we didn't see the things again until a year later. Living by the sea, I went fishing a lot, and enjoyed the myriad ways local cooks worked magic with our local seafood. As in other parts of Scandinavia, much of this magic involved delicate techniques of smoking and curing.

I remember the wonderful flavors of my childhood as though they were yesterday, not 30 years ago. And those flavors still guide me, still inspire me, as much as my travels far beyond Finland (even to a strange place called Houston, Texas) have enriched what I'm able to cook.

I think I was about 10 when my aunt, Anne-Marie Rantala, became Anne-Marie Rantala-Ragazzini—a mouthful, to be sure. She moved with her husband to a tiny village called Godo in Emilia-Romagna, just a few miles up from the town of Ravenna, famous for its churches full of Byzantine mosaics. Anne-Marie's life wasn't about mosaics, though. It was about cooking for her family. As I discovered during her trips home to Finland or several years later on my first visit to Godo, that meant starting every day at her 200-year-old family house with a decision: what to serve for lunch and what to serve for dinner, followed by a long string of trips to the garden just outside and to various markets and street vendors in the village. There were, of course, no supermarkets around Godo in those days, just individuals and families doing what they had been doing for hundreds of years. Yes, some of that way of life still existed in Pori, or in smaller towns in Finland, but I had seen nothing like what I saw in Italy. And I'd tasted nothing like what I tasted there, either.

You might say my first job (unpaid, naturally) was as Anne-Marie's sous chef. Not only did I help her with meals whenever she was home in Pori and when I visited her in Godo, but I made meals for my family in her style and in her stead. I'd started cooking Finnish dishes with my

grandmother when I was as young as 3 and a lot of foods with my mom in the years after that, but by the time I'd gotten Italian food in my blood, my fate in the kitchen was sealed.

As most people should know by now, loving to cook and deciding to make your living in the grueling restaurant business are two different things. By high school, I was beginning to understand myself a little, along with the things I liked and was good at. I was, generally, good with my hands, so that pointed me toward crafts like carpentry. But I was also good with languages, picking up Swedish and even English without much trouble. So that pointed me toward one of Finland's university programs. Still, my love of cooking overruled any and all other interests. And I was happy to let it overrule.

As soon as I completed high school and my 11 months of service in the army, I applied to culinary school in Turku, a city about 150 miles south of Pori. And, even though the study itself was grueling, I was already too eager to sit still when I wasn't in cooking class. I visited a restaurant in Turku called Julia, which had just been voted Finland's restaurant of the year, and I talked my way into a hard-working apprenticeship. In America, I know, they'd probably call this an "externship" (a made-up word, I'm pretty sure), but in Europe we have a strong tradition of apprenticeship in all crafts and trades. So that's what I became on my days off from culinary school, a culinary apprentice. On any given day, I can't tell you where I learned the most.

The chefs at Restaurant Julia, you see, did everything the hardcore, old-fashioned way, tolerating no compromises and definitely (since I was the guy who had to do the worst jobs) no shortcuts. Stocks and sauces were our heart and soul, and I learned the slowest, hardest and best ways to make them all. Everything we sent out of that kitchen was made by our own hands. As different as the food was from anything in Godo, Aunt Anne-Marie would have felt right at home.

As in the best resumes, or maybe just the luckiest, my apprenticeship throughout the two-year program turned into my very first job. I'd already done everything at Restaurant Julia as well as at its sister operation called the Marina Palace, so taking me on as an employee seemed

the most natural thing in the world. But I was still hungry to see and taste and learn, especially now from other chefs, chefs who did different things different ways. I wasn't yet married with children back then, in the mid-nineties, so I was free to spend my days off any way I pleased. And how I pleased was in other chefs' kitchens, holding down stations, peeling potatoes, whatever. David would probably say I was a chef tournant, a chef who "turns" through any kitchen job that needs filling, but really, it was my idea of fun. I traveled a lot around Finland, including to Helsinki, and saw a lot of things I could do someday when I had a restaurant of my own. All the same, the path to that point wasn't clear to me yet, since a chef's humble paycheck doesn't exactly turn anyone into an entrepreneur/business owner overnight. It would take one truly unexpected encounter several years later to accomplish that.

One day, I spotted a newspaper want ad for a chef at the Royal Danish Embassy in Helsinki. I went after it because it sounded like a great place to learn, and I started cooking there on my 25th birthday. You definitely remember birthdays like that. I did parties for hundreds of people on a regular basis, people who included princes and princesses from Denmark, as well as business, political and social leaders from all over Europe. It was a good job, but eventually I moved on to a small hotel near Turku and, after a year there, on to another spa hotel not far away. At that second spa, I actually got to work on equal footing, even though I was still in my twenties, with the master chefs who had taught me so much back at Restaurant Julia.

If newspaper ads have often carried me away, lured me from one job to the next, in the spring of 2000 it was a newspaper ad that brought me home. It was a real estate ad this time, for a 1920s house by the sea, 16 miles from Pori. By then I was married to my wife, Sani, so any decision wasn't mine alone. But we visited that house by the sea and it was love at first sight. We wanted to move in that very day. There was only one small problem: I didn't have a job in my hometown, a way to pay our bills. And at that time, Pori didn't have any restaurants that operated at the level that would let me do the things I believed in, or that would pay me what places elsewhere were willing and able to pay me. It seemed impossible, really, until I met a man who owned a nightclub in Pori and wanted to create a restaurant as part of it. By the end of three days of talking, that man told me, "Go to the bank and buy the house. Let's make a restaurant."

In another stroke of good fortune, only three days before we opened the place we named P.K. Cabinet, I competed in a national chefs competition and won third place, winning over dozens of tough chefs from the big city, Helsinki. This made quite a splash, considering my youth and relative anonymity. Everybody wanted to know who I was and where I cooked, and I was more than happy to tell them. I worked as the head chef at P.K. Cabinet for three and a half years, marking the first time I'd been officially in charge of a commercial kitchen. It even led to plans for my first of two cookbooks written and published in Finnish. More importantly, by 2004, it led to the unexpected meeting that gave me Bucco.

I was meeting with the head of a local dairy about his sponsoring my first cookbook, and that part went fine; he agreed to do so within an hour. But then he led me to a part of his building on the river that had been empty for more than two years. Even in its less-than-perfect condition, the space had a clean, contemporary look, and I loved the wide windows that opened onto the river. Within minutes, I told him I wanted to create my own restaurant in the space. And I did.

Beginning in June of 2004, Pori wasn't just my hometown anymore. It was a place where I owned a business, not to mention a place where I raised a family, first in that wonderful house by the sea and later in a bigger place in town. We started a family in 1999 with my daughter Anna, while still living in Turku. But it continued in 2001 with my son, Eemeli, and then in 2004 with another daughter, Aino. Sani loves to tease me about the connection between having a new baby and launching a new

restaurant. Big new chapters in my career began in 1999 and 2001, so when Aino came along in 2004, my wife asked me what my trouble was: why wasn't I opening a new restaurant? Six days later, I found Bucco.

I loved the space pretty much as it was, a very good thing when you don't have a ton of money for renovations. And since it had been the dairy's staff restaurant before closing, it had a solid kitchen I could more or less use as is, at least in the beginning.

As a business owner, I came to see Pori in a new light. The place has many things going for it. In addition to its own 80,000 residents, it enjoys a brisk tourism industry, especially (this being Finland) in the lovely summertime, when it stays light outside almost around the clock. Finns and everyone who visits love to make the most of that, enjoying activities along our river (the Kokemaen), at the largest beach in Scandinavia and during our Jazz Festival that's been going on since 1966. It's crazy to think about, but our Jazz Festival is four years older than the one held each year in New Orleans!

From the beginning, I wanted Bucco to be the embodiment of everything I believed about food, going back to that visit to Godo when I was 10. It would have to be comfortable for our guests, with no pomposity or intimidation. It would be about how good food can be when you start with perfect local ingredients in season and then try like hell not to mess them up. We wanted to serve good wines at a fair price, so I added a vinoteca to our ristorante, a fun-casual wine bar that would serve us well for small meetings and private parties.

At any given time at Bucco, our menu is more than half Italian, those classic Italian favorites that Finns love every bit as much as their counterparts in America, who regularly vote Italian their favorite cuisine. One of our all-time signature dishes, one of those items you can't take off the menu without rioting in the streets, is our vitello tonnato. We feel we make one of the best versions anywhere of this appetizer (thin slices of veal in lemon-kissed tuna sauce with capers), and more than a few Italians have stepped forward to agree. At the other end of the meal, dessert, it's our spin on zuppa inglese (yes, it does mean "English soup")

that rules the roost. To my taste, a lot of restaurants make zuppa inglese too sweet. Ours is all about balance, with Chantilly cream with liqueur, layered with Savoyard cookies and chocolate mousse, then topped with Italian meringue toasted with a torch. It's four layers, and I encourage my guests to get a little of each layer in every spoonful.

Over the years, as my reputation as a chef grew and my wanderlust failed to subside, I was able to travel throughout Europe, tasting and borrowing something from virtually every mile. From the French, I picked up roasting chicken with fresh tarragon and a creamy sauce of cognac and forest mushrooms. From the Spanish, I learned to take gravlax (the cured salmon beloved all over Scandinavia) and outfit it with a crisp mosaic salad of vegetables, olive oil and white balsamic vinegar. I even picked up a trick or two from the Russians, inspiring me to feature a selection of blinis at Bucco. Now that's traveling a long way from tiny Godo. And of course, we serve several Scandinavian traditional dishes; some of the best involve smoked white tail deer. That's what makes it so intriguing, me writing a cookbook with a chef in Texas. There can be no question that smoked meats are a Texas thing. Except, I suppose, when they're a Scandinavian thing. David and I believe in connections. We don't believe in boundaries.

After several years of operating Bucco successfully, I've come to believe what I always suspected: a restaurant isn't about the furniture, the stove or the plates. It's really about the good stuff that you make from your heart. In my heart, I've made Le Mistral "my restaurant" in North America, with all the connections I feel to the way David creates his flavors. This is the food I feel and taste. This is the food that comes from my heart. In an Italian restaurant like Bucco or a French one like Le Mistral, with every portion for every guest, you have to give a piece of your heart.

This is the food I feel and taste. This is the food that comes from my heart. In an Italian restaurant like Bucco or a French one like Le Mistral, with every portion for every guest, you have to give a piece of your heart.

Over two weeks in March 2010, David and Jani paid a visit to each other's homelands, accompanied by writer John DeMers and photographer Shannon O'Hara. The result here is a kind of verbal travel diary, a spirited and ongoing conversation about food and drink, tradition and innovation, history and family.

ICE HOCKEY, VEGETABLES AND BEER

JANI: I am afraid that people think that all we chefs do is cook and eat, with side trips to go shop for things in order to cook and eat. Tonight I

wanted to offer my guests in Finland a chance for some rigorous physical activity. So it was time for a sport we've always loved in my country, ice hockey.

DAVID: But Jani, we went to a hockey game. That means we ate some vegetables and salad, drank draft beers and sat in our seats for something like three hours.

J: As I said, rigorous physical activity. We love our hockey team in Pori, and they've been the national champions of Finland twice, in 1971 and 1978. The team colors are red and black, and our team is called the Assat. You know—

D: The what? Assat?

J: Yes, of course. Assat. Like the playing card? The assat of spades.

D: Oh, I see. The Aces.

J: If you say so. The Pori Aces. We love our Aces. And this is a big game. They have to win if they want to keep playing.

D: I think, Jani, that in America they'd call this the playoffs. But really, let's talk about the food served at the game first, upstairs in the VIP Room. I thought it was very good. Vegetables, simple vegetables. Only potatoes and carrots, but they had a lot of good flavor.

J: That's from the curry and the cream. I wasn't going to have anything, except maybe a beer or perhaps some apple cider. But you're going on and on about these vegetables. So even though we are going for a small supper at Bucco after the game, I try a plate. And no, the vegetables are not so bad at all.

D: I have seconds. Perhaps thirds. And Jani, how did you arrange for it to snow today, this morning, to welcome us to Finland? You said it was becoming springtime here already. That it was hot, that we would be wearing only our shirt sleeves. In America, I think they would call this a freak snowstorm.

J: In Finland, I'm not sure we would ever call a snowstorm that.

D: But it is very beautiful. The streets were all dark and dirty and gray when we arrived. And now look, Jani, everything is perfectly white.

J: And it makes the light so lovely in my restaurant along the river. You will sleep well in Finland tonight, my friend.

D: After arriving at 3:30 this morning, after missing our connection at Heathrow and staying an extra seven hours there till the next flight, I think I'd sleep well almost anywhere.

J: You should have another beer. And it's the start of the third period. We'd better get back in there and cheer for Assat. Because you see, it is time for us to have some more rigorous physical activity. That is what we love here in Finland.

A STEAMY LATE AFTERNOON

JANI: Everyone who comes to visit Finland has to try a sauna, like you did this afternoon. I hear you have saunas in the States, but from what I can tell, they wouldn't impress anyone from Finland. They're steambaths, maybe. But true Finnish saunas, not at all.

DAVID: What, I have to beat myself with branches or something?

J: Some people do, of course. It is part of a very old tradition. But you and I both know that owning a restaurant is punishment enough. So no, this afternoon, you didn't have to beat yourself with anything. But you had to spend some time in a true, old-fashioned sauna—like the 75-year-old one my friend Ilkka Haaslahti has right on the shore of the Baltic Sea. And then, if you're lucky, Ilkka will cut a hole in the ice and throw you in. That's quite invigorating.

D: Today, though, the ice was dangerous because it's starting to melt with spring. So Ilkka couldn't throw me in. Now that's what I call lucky! The sauna, though, was excellent. It was surprising in many ways.

J: I told you it would be. You just sit there on that bench naked, drinking a cold beer, and every so often I'll use a long kind of ladle to pour water onto the hot coals. The room fills with very hot steam.

D: Burning hot steam—

J: And that's what makes saunas so healthy, you see. If you have any impurities left in your body after a true Finnish sauna, well, you're probably about to die.

D: After some of those steam attacks of yours, I'm a little surprised I have any skin left. And I had to close my eyes each time too, because otherwise I figured you were trying to burn them out of their sockets.

J: Close your eyes and think about the meaning of life, my friend. That's what we do in Finland all the time.

D: A sure sign of a winter that's too long. At least there's another bucket in the sauna, for dousing your body with cool water when you just get too overheated. I haven't sweated that much since I was doing all the hard, dirty work they give an apprentice in the kitchen.

J: It's good to remember our humble beginnings, David.

D: Maybe not so much.

J: And then, when we'd had enough sauna—and since Ilkka wasn't able to throw us into the sea—we wrapped a towel around where it mattered and stepped outside to finish our beers on the veranda. You might think it would be cold outside, but it didn't feel that way after the sauna, did it?

D: No, amazingly, it didn't feel cold. But there had to be some deep meaning in the way the steam was coming off our bodies like smoke from a forest fire. I'm not a scientist, but I'm sure that said something about the temperature difference from the sauna to the world of late winter on the west coast of Finland.

J: Well, yeah, probably. But then we went inside Ilkka's house to fix dinner.

D: Your sauna menu was intriguing. It included a lot of things that seemed true to Finland—native, I mean. Things we don't eat back in France, and definitely not in the United States.

J: As they say in English, don't look a gift horse in the mouth.

D: Yes, but you shouldn't cook him for dinner, either.

J: Come on, David. There was no horse. And you French people have no room to talk—from the place that taught the world to think snails were food.

D: It was an excellent menu, Jani. I especially enjoyed your main course, the wild duck breast and risotto with wild duck-leg confit.

J: You just like duck confit.

D: I do like duck confit. But there were other new things to try as well, from slightly familiar ideas like cured fillet of venison with a salad of brown chanterelle mushrooms and crème fraîche, to the heart of young moose. Can't say that would be a huge seller back in Texas.

J: Of course, David, but you have to admit it was good. The heart is a muscle, not an organ, so it tastes a lot like a steak, which definitely would sell back in Texas. And naturally, for a Finnish sauna menu on the shores of the Baltic Sea, we couldn't sit down to eat even a snack without some fish. We had warm smoked salmon, smoked whitefish, pickled herring and some nice salmon eggs.

D: I could probably sell salmon eggs in Texas—as long as I billed them as caviar.

J: When they taste as great as these did, you can bill them any way you like.

JANI: Two ways we chefs have of keeping up with who is doing what in our industry—

DAVID: And sometimes who is cooking what, Jani.

J: Yes, exactly. Two of the ways we keep up with trends in our industry are going to trade shows, which usually involve a great deal of wine tasting, and going out to dine in each other's restaurants. And since, this time, that means traveling from my Pori to Helsinki and having dinner at my friend Hans Välimäki's two–Michelin starred restaurant, Chez Dominique, it's not such a bad deal. It also makes it a little easier to get up at 4:45 in the morning for our flight tomorrow to the South of France.

D: I'm not sure when getting up at 4:45 in the morning got to be easier than anything. I am a French chef, you know.

J: I know, David. But I think it's worth it. In Helsinki, the wine expo and gastronomic show have a lot of meaning for me. It's an excellent trade show, for one thing. And there is the big chef's competition, the only time each year I get to visit all my chef friends from the restaurants in the capital. Back in 2001, I came in third out of 12 finalists, the only one of the 12 from outside Helsinki. All the guys, even this year, are good friends of mine.

D: But Jani, it seems to me that this year all the chefs look like children. I know they call them "young chefs" and that, especially at the more creative restaurants, having a "young chef" is all the rage everywhere. But don't you think all that smooth baby skin on the faces was rubbing it in a bit?

J: We have good skin here in Finland. I think it's all the saunas we take.

D: I am pretty sure some of those guys today aren't even shaving yet.

J: Speak for yourself, Chef. Still, between seeing who gets to be the best chef in all of Finland this year—judged by his peers—and tasting some wines I haven't been able to try yet, it was well worth spending the day in the big city.

D: It was very interesting. Helsinki is such a beautiful city. And besides, I'm thinking that every time I lost you for a while in the exhibition center, all I had to do was look in the champagne section. It was enough to make a Frenchman's heart break out in the "Marseillaise." In fact, I believe I will sing it for you right now.

J: If you do that, I'll have to do "Finlandia." And I mean all the verses. And besides, this was me you're talking about, the chef from Bucco. I couldn't stay away from the Italian wines for very long. I tasted the 2005 Solaia from Antinori, and in Finland that was so allocated that the only way to get even one bottle was by lottery. And I enjoyed the Tignanello of 2006 as well.

D: And then, after a full day of tasting wines on the hall floor and hopefully not ending up on the hall floor—

J: An occupational hazard, I think you Americans say.

D: Yes, after that, we had all those wonderful courses at Chez Dominique. I'm not sure how many courses we even had, Jani, since there were at least three amuses bouches before the meal even started to get serious.

J: Your bouche was amused, I hope.

D: Yes, very. Some of the dishes—the fish course of Atlantic halibut perfectly poached, the beef tenderloin—really, Jani, some of your friend's

dishes really blew me away. And the staff was amazing. I was surprised by how many of the servers were not from Finland, including the one guy from England and the one guy from France. I think everything was top-notch. In particular, I wanted to take the dishes home to Le Mistral.

J: Well, we all share ideas—

D: No, Jani. In this case, I don't mean the culinary dishes. I mean the dishes: those wonderful curving white plates. If I could slip them into my luggage and take them home to Le Revest tomorrow, and after that then home to Houston, I think I would. Is that so wrong of me?

J: Chef Hans might frown upon it, even with all his cookbooks and his two Michelin stars.

D: It's settled then. The dishes stay here in Helsinki. You know I wouldn't want to do anything to make the chef frown.

COOKING SUNSHINE

DAVID: Jani, do you know when I knew I wasn't in Finland anymore—when I knew I was home?

JANI: When you could peel off your heavy coat outside the airport in the sunshine?

D: Of course. But when I really knew was when I tasted the pissaladière that my cousin Sylvia set out for us outside beside the pool at her home.

J: A kind of pizza, yes? It was very good. As though the pizza sneaked over into Provence from Italy, just a few miles of Mediterranean coastline away?

D: Yes, quite similar to pizza, but very old, very ancient. Besides, Jani, how do we know the pissaladière didn't sneak across the border into Italy, huh? I think it could have happened. But either way, it is one of the authentic tastes of Provence—or rather, it is many authentic tastes, all in one. The crusty, chewy bread underneath, of course, made with olive oil and salt. And the layer of caramelized onions of top, and all of that spread with anchovies and black Niçoise olives. To some, of course, the taste of my home is the salade Niçoise, which has similarities with the tuna fresh from the fisherman. But to me, I know I am home when I taste the pissaladière.

J: And speaking of fishermen, the visit to the market was a beautiful thing this morning. We had to get the fish to cook for your family tonight. But we also, when we weren't stopping for a café and of course a pastis, needed fresh vegetables to make for dinner.

D: The Saturday market at Sanery-sur-Mer was amazing, Jani. So much color, and so much flavor. The lady we bought many things from, you know, she was telling me that several of her vegetables had still been in the ground this morning, that they were picked right before she came to the market. The Italian parsley—that, she said, had been growing only 45 minutes before we bought it. That's why it was just lying in the crate behind her table, not yet sorted into bunches.

J: And then, David, there were the au pairs you also picked out—

D: No, really, I don't think I can do that. But it was nice, when I was talking to the lady with all the candied fruit and that wonderful garlic. She told me she wished she could send her two daughters to the States to live with me and my family for a few months—to work as au pairs with my children and to definitely improve their English. It seemed strange, since she did not know me. She said I seemed like a very kind man.

J: I hope you told her you're a chef. She obviously doesn't know you as well as I do.

D: And once we'd filled our basket with vegetables and picked out some rascasse—it's similar to a sea bass—and then two fresh rabbits from the butcher, we strolled along the waterfront looking at the traditional fishing boats. I love the way their sails are tilted—their masts, would you say?—like graceful razors cutting through the air in the sunshine. They remind me that the ancient Romans are never very far away in Provence, or even

the ancient Greeks, who pretty much named all the places we go around here. And that the Egyptians, even back in history, lived just across the street—the street being the Mediterranean, which says everything about who we are and how we live. And especially about how we eat.

J: I love just saying that word: rascasse!

D: And what you did with it, Jani, wrapping it in cabbage leaves, made everyone in my family say the word over and over again tonight. You people in Finland love your cabbage rolls.

J: Yes. We call them kaalikääryleet, if you don't mind repeating after me. Really, the dish was very simple, just the bright green of the blanched cabbage leaves opening into, once you cut it, the white of the fish and the little rainbow of the carrots, shallots, fennel and celery, all tied together with a light beurre monte. I'd actually never made this dish before, David. It's just something that came to me as we walked through the market.

D: And then, for our entrée, we made the lapin a la Provençal—well, perhaps everything we cooked tonight might be called Provençal.

J: But the lapin was incredible.

D: And very simple, just like your fish. My family—my mother and her friend Gilbert, my cousin Sylvia and her husband, Gilles, their friends Frederique and Pascale, who grow grapes and make wonderful wines here in Bandol, and of course the children, Estelle, Emelie and Robin—really loved the rabbit we fixed.

J: We served the lapin as a kind of rustic stew, with olives and garlic, plus candied carambola from the lady with the au pair daughters, a small stick of cinnamon borrowed from North Africa—across the street, as you would say—and a bit of brandy flavored with almonds.

D: It looked so good on the plate beside the ratatouille, and you can't get any more Provençal than that, even after that movie. In the States, you know, I sometimes see chefs make ratatouille and it's all about the tomato, as though maybe it's some kind of Italian pasta sauce.

J: We are very close to Italy here, David. I taste both Italy and France in this dish.

D: Yes, Jani, so do I. But also, no. Ratatouille is about the fresh vegetables and about cooking them separately so each one is done perfectly. The eggplant, of course, you have to cook last because it is like a sponge. It sucks up all the olive oil, takes it away from everything else if you try to cook the whole thing together. This way, the vegetables are perfect and the colors are deep and bright at the same time.

J: We served the lapin over that special polenta you made, speaking of Italy, with bacon and onions and plenty of Parmesan cheese, and that excellent tomato coulis from your cousin's husband, Gilles. He assured us he put nothing in the jar but tomato.

D: But I think he lied just a little bit, Jani. I'm sure there was sunshine in the jar, too.

J: And at the very end, you spread the polenta on a sheet pan, covered it with more cheese and turned it golden under the broiler. You gratinéed it, we chefs would say.

D: I think back in Texas, I'd have to call that "pizza grits." Or maybe "grits du pizza."

J: Yes, my friend. Back in Texas, I think you just might have to do that.

BEAUTY AND THE BOUILLABAISSE

DAVID: Today, Jani, we visited one of the most beautiful villages in what we call deep Provence—the part that's inland from all the craziness of the Côte d'Azur.

JANI: The French Riviera.

D: Yes, exactly. Le Castellet, as we saw, is a long way from all that. Except in the summer, when it has so many tourists, the town on top of the mountain is very quiet, almost silent sometimes, with only a few church bells ringing. It became Le Castellet in the Middle Ages, when everything was about protection—thick walls, heavy gates they could close, and of course a location high above the valley with a perfect view in all directions. It was easy to defend from all the bad guys.

J: You know, I was reminded, especially walking up those narrow stone streets—I'm glad that cars are not allowed, by the way—I was reminded of the same kinds of towns in Italy. Built for defense. Beautiful places like Assisi and Orvieto, which not surprisingly make some very good wines. In the ancient times, it wasn't about la dolce vita, though; it was about staying alive. Way back when all the Italian city-states were going to war with each other every other week, like one big eternal football match. Final score: Perugia 4, Ferrara 1.

D: *Plus ça change,* Jani.

J: But then, David, we came down to the sea again, to enjoy some bouillabaisse. That was very interesting to me, since I know the fish soups and seafood stews of Italy, as well as the ones we have back home in Finland. In the north of Italy—along the coasts, of course, before refrigeration let them move fish inland—zuppa di pesce is often made with cheap rockfish. You get a nice broth, with tomato and basil and seasonings, and then maybe you throw the fish away because they have so little meat. That wouldn't work when the dish made its way to America and became cioppino.

D: The Americans would insist on using more expensive fish.

J: So now cioppino, like they serve in San Francisco, is all about eating the fish—the snapper, the calamari, the shrimp, the scallops, whatever the chef can find that's freshest and best.

D: And in Finland, Jani—

J: We actually have seasonal fish soups, similar to these others in most ways but using what we are catching at specific times of the year. Some of our fish soups and stews produce their own clear broth, and others are made with cream. In the winter and spring, when it's still cold in Finland and there's still snow and ice on the ground and even on the frozen sea, these dishes are very good at warming you up.

D: And you know, Jani, bouillabaisse used to have more in common with all of those than people might think, now that it's one of the most famous dishes from Marseille and the rest of Provence. Today, it's very expensive to make at home and even more expensive to buy in a restaurant on the waterfront, but in the beginning it was very cheap fisherman's food.

J: They sold everyone else the good stuff, the fillets—

D: Yes. And kept the heads and tails and bones for themselves, to feed their families. Originally, they used whatever they had and gave the broth flavor with tomato, saffron (which also wasn't all that expensive in those days) and a kind of very garlicky mayonnaise called rouille in Provence.

J: After eating that, you must excuse my breath.

D: This is Provence, Jani. No one will even notice. But eventually, after many centuries of fishermen making this old-fashioned dish, the fish you can use in a true bouillabaisse, like the one we had for lunch today, became set in stone. No matter how expensive they get, you just have to use them. The people of Provence would be horrified if they came to America and saw all this bouillabaisse being made with red snapper and scallops and whatever. As the owner showed us before he cooked, the real thing must be made with rascasse, gaulinette, rouget, St. Pierre, groudin, conger, favouille and calamar.

J: I can guess what calamar is. But can you please translate the rest into English?

D: No. But I guess we could look it up.

J: On your iPhone?

D: Naturally.

J: It is like with the wines in France. Every time you French do anything with a wine, there is some kind of holy law that tells you how to do it. These are the grapes you must use, this is what must happen to the grapes, this is how they must be described on the label. What is it about you French guys and all your laws, David?

D: We are French. We love to make laws, to write them in large books, the more laws the better. It is a shame, perhaps, that we don't very much like to follow them.

Le Mistral Recipes

1¼ pounds deveined uncooked foie gras

½ teaspoon sea salt

⅛ teaspoon white pepper

¼ cup Sauternes wine

1 quart duck stock *(see recipe p. 184)*

1 cheesecloth, cut 2 to 3 inches wide and 10 to 16 inches long

1 thick kitchen towel

kitchen string

Foie Gras au Torchon

Serves 8 to 10

This dish pairs so well with toasted butter brioche that we've decided to include the recipe right afterwards. A glass of Sauternes is also an excellent touch.

Place the piece of foie gras in a bowl. Season with salt, pepper and Sauternes. Let marinate in the refrigerator for 6 to 8 hours. Roll it tightly in the cheesecloth. Tightly bind both ends with kitchen string. Repeat the same operation using the kitchen towel and tightly tie both ends again.

Put duck stock in a large pot over high heat. Reduce the heat as soon as it boils. Place the foie gras in cheese cloth into the duck stock for about 8 to 10 minutes. Slowly remove the poached foie gras from the stock.

Gently tilt up the foie gras to drain the extra fat onto a plate; discard the fat. Cut five 20-inch pieces of kitchen string and tie the string evenly around the foie gras torchon. Refrigerate for 24 hours before serving.

To serve, remove foie gras from refrigerator and slice to desired thickness. Do not forget to remove the cloth on every slice before serving with Small Butter Brioche.

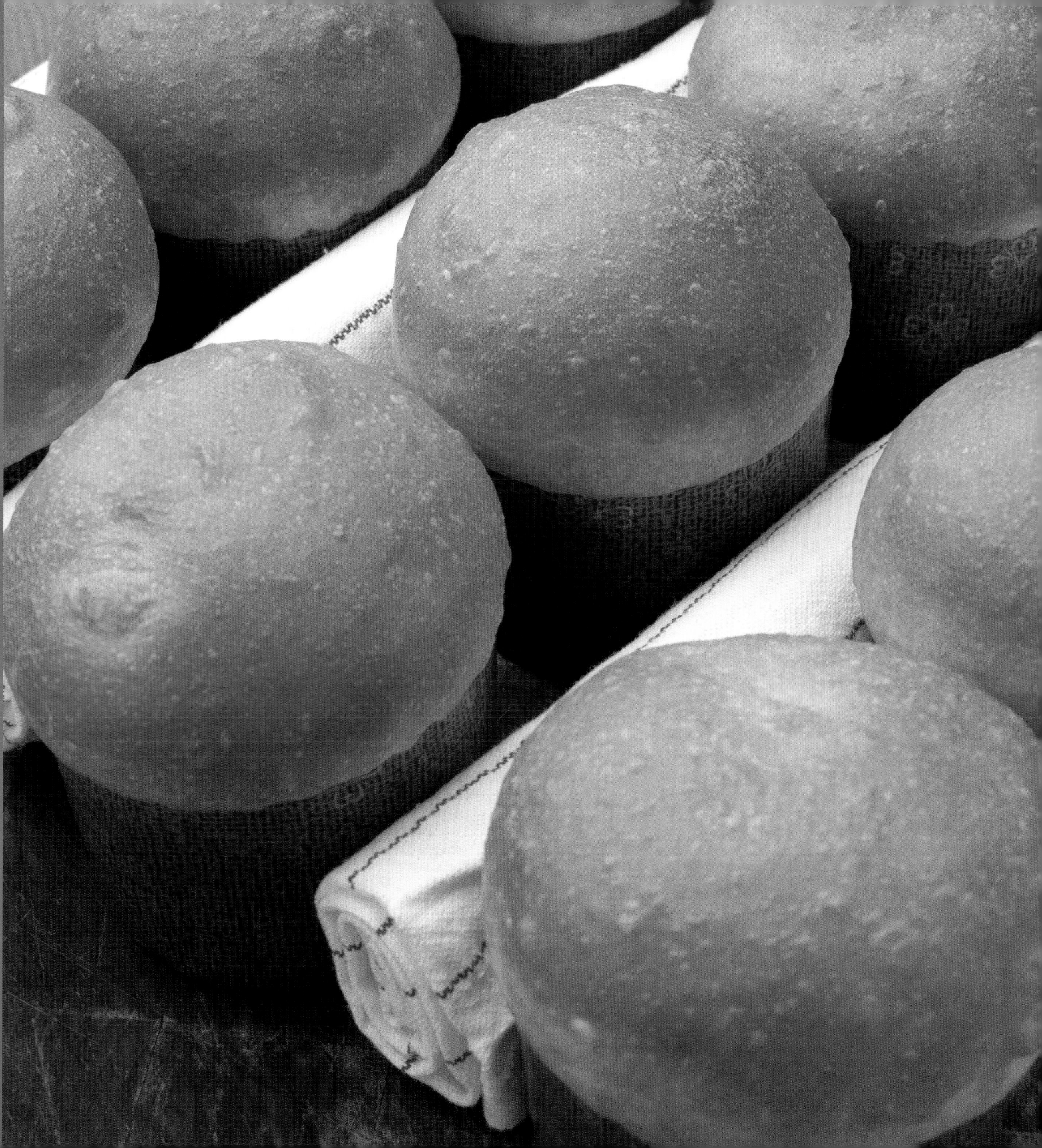

½ ounce baker's yeast

(It looks like a cube. You will find it in the dairy department of the grocery store. Do not use powdered yeast.)

¾ cup whole milk

3 cups all-purpose flour

1 tablespoon sugar

⅛ teaspoon salt

2 eggs

¾ cup (1½ sticks) unsalted butter, at room temperature

Small Butter Brioche

Serves 6

These brioches are fun all by themselves—think of them as oh-so–French dinner rolls. But they are especially wonderful with our foie gras dish.

Preheat the oven to 350° F.

Butter the inside of 6 round bread molds or a large muffin tin and sprinkle with flour. Put yeast in a small bowl and cover with milk to dissolve it. Then combine yeast with all the ingredients except butter in the bowl of an electric mixer. Mix slowly and as soon as the dough becomes consistent, forming a ball, keep mixing slowly and add butter gradually. Incorporating the butter into the dough should take about 12 minutes.

Form dough into 6 balls and place them in molds or muffin tin. Set aside in a warm place to rise, about 45 minutes to an hour. Once the dough rises to about half the size of the mold, put in the oven to bake for 10 to 15 minutes, until golden. Remove from the oven and let cool.

MARINADE:

½ cup Provençal pastis

2 tablespoons extra-virgin olive oil

2 tablespoons chopped fresh dill

2 tablespoons chopped fresh cilantro

SHRIMP:

18 jumbo shrimp, peeled and deveined

2 tablespoons chopped fresh cilantro

Salt and pepper

SAUCE:

1 tablespoon extra-virgin olive oil

2 zucchini, chopped

1 tablespoon finely chopped shallot

1 tablespoon chopped fresh cilantro

3 cups chicken stock (see recipe p. 184)

2 tablespoons lemon juice

Salt and pepper

FENNEL CONFIT:

¼ cup plus 2 tablespoons extra-virgin olive oil

2 heads fresh fennel root, thinly sliced

1 clove garlic

1 bay leaf

½ teaspoon fennel powder

Salt and pepper

Grilled Jumbo Shrimp in Pastis with Lemon Zucchini Sauce

Serves 6

In Provence, one of the most popular tastes belongs to the licorice-flavored spirit called pastis. If you know Pernod or Herbsaint, you get the general idea. But if you want to make this a true Provençal dish, you'll need to arm-wrestle Jani for real pastis.

Put all marinade ingredients in a large bowl. Marinate shrimp in this mixture overnight in the refrigerator.

Make the sauce by cooking the zucchini and shallot in olive oil over low heat for 15 to 20 minutes, until tender. At the last minute, add cilantro. Transfer the vegetables to a blender and pour in chicken stock and lemon juice; blend until smooth. Pass the sauce through a fine sieve. Season to taste with salt and pepper. Keep warm.

Prepare the fennel confit by heating the olive oil in a sauté pan. Add the fennel, garlic, bay leaf, salt and pepper to taste and fennel powder. Cook over low heat until fennel is tender and transparent, about 20 minutes.

Salt and pepper the marinated shrimp. Grill shrimp for 5 minutes on each side. Sprinkle with cilantro. To serve, place the fennel confit on plates and cover with the shrimp. Serve the zucchini sauce on the side to show the nice red color of the shrimp.

Duck Confit with Fingerling Mashed Potatoes and King Trumpet Mushrooms

Serves 4

Making duck confit is relatively easy—or at least relatively foolproof—though most Americans have only been aware of the technique for a decade or less. Several companies market good duck confit via gourmet shops, if you insist on taking a shortcut.

Prepare the confit by seasoning the duck legs with the salt and pepper; let sit in the refrigerator for 2 to 3 hours. Rinse the duck, removing some of the salt and pepper. Put duck and all remaining confit ingredients into a large stock pot, cover and cook over low heat for 3 hours. Remove and debone the legs. Shred the meat.

Put the potatoes in a large saucepot and cover with water. Season the water with the salt and pepper. Once the water comes to a boil, let the potatoes cook for approximately 15 minutes, or until very tender. Drain and mash the potatoes with the olive oil, using a hand masher or fork.

To make the sauce, melt 1 tablespoon of the butter in a large sauté pan and sweat the shallots. Add peppercorns, bay leaf and thyme. Cook until golden brown, about 5 minutes. Deglaze with Sauternes, reducing until syrupy. Slowly melt the remaining butter into the sauce. Season with salt and pepper. Pass through a fine sieve.

Cut the mushrooms in half lengthwise and pan sear in butter in a sauté pan until golden brown, about 4 minutes on each side. Fill the bottom half of a 2-inch ring mold with mashed potatoes, followed by a layer of duck confit. Carefully lift off the mold and place the mushroom on top. Drizzle the sauce around it. Garnish with thyme leaves.

DUCK CONFIT:

2 pounds duck legs
1 tablespoon salt
½ teaspoon black pepper
1 teaspoon minced garlic
1 bay leaf
1 teaspoon chopped fresh rosemary
1 quart warmed duck fat

FINGERLING MASHED POTATOES:

1 pound fingerling potatoes,
  cut in half lengthwise
1 teaspoon salt
1 teaspoon black pepper
1½ teaspoons extra-virgin olive oil

SAUCE:

4 tablespoons (1/2 stick) unsalted butter
1 shallot, thinly sliced
2 black peppercorns
1 bay leaf
1 sprig thyme
1½ cups Sauternes wine
1½ teaspoons salt
½ teaspoon white pepper

KING TRUMPET MUSHROOMS:

2 king trumpet mushrooms
1 tablespoon unsalted butter
2 sprigs thyme, for garnish

SCALLOPS:

8 Hawaiian sea scallops

Sea salt and pepper

¼ cup extra-virgin olive oil

MARINADE:

1 tablespoon chopped fresh tarragon

Juice of 1 lime

1 tablespoon diced celery

2 tablespoons diced cucumber

2 tablespoons diced fennel root

2 tablespoons white balsamic vinegar

2 tablespoons plus 2 teaspoons salmon eggs

1 tablespoon chopped fresh chives, to garnish

Hawaiian Scallops
with Cucumber Fennel Salmon-Egg Ceviche

Serves 4

The greatest contribution Japanese cuisine has made to America is our increased awareness of seafood that's not overcooked. Once we opened the door to sushi, in other words, a thousand versions of ceviche and other delights strolled right on in.

Season the scallops with sea salt and pepper to taste. Drizzle some olive oil on top. Set the oven to broil position. Place the scallops in the oven and broil for about 2 minutes. Let cool and set in the refrigerator.

Mix all the marinade ingredients together in a large bowl and let sit for 1 hour in the refrigerator. Pour marinade on the scallops before serving. Sprinkle chives over the scallops for garnish. Serve immediately.

Note: This dish needs to be served extremely cold. The scallops probably won't be cooked through after only 2 minutes of broiling. Don't worry about it; the acidity of the ceviche marinade will finish the cooking process.

Mistral Salad with Blueberry-Balsamic Vinaigrette

Serves 6 to 8

VINAIGRETTE:

1   cup fresh blueberries

2   tablespoons sugar

1   teaspoon Dijon mustard

½   cup balsamic vinegar

1   cup vegetable oil

1   cup extra-virgin olive oil

Salt and pepper

SALAD:

6   cups spring mix

¼   cup toasted pine nuts

2   tablespoons toasted sesame seeds

18   sprigs chives, to garnish

1   sprig chervil, to garnish

Every day and every night, this is our best-selling salad at Le Mistral—thus the name. My guess is that people love the way the tangy blueberry vinaigrette spotlights the unexpected crunch of the pine nuts and sesame seeds.

To make the vinaigrette, cook the blueberries and sugar in a small saucepan over low heat for 20 to 25 minutes, until very soft. Set aside to cool. Whisk together mustard, vinegar and blueberries. Slowly pour in the oils, whisking constantly. Season to taste with salt and pepper.

Put the spring mix in a large bowl, add 1 cup of vinaigrette and toss gently. Use a ring mold or dough cutter to shape the salad on each individual plate. Sprinkle with toasted pine nuts and sesame seeds. Garnish with chives and chervil.

2   anchovy fillets

3   tablespoons balsamic vinegar

¼   cup extra-virgin olive oil

SALAD:

About 72 grape tomatoes (1½ pounds),
    mix of 3 colors

2   tablespoons chopped fresh parsley

2   tablespoons chopped fresh basil

Half a shallot, minced

Salt and pepper

Three Grape–Tomato Salad

Serves 6

The border between France and Italy is erased with this wonderful summertime tomato salad, as it is in my family tree.

To prepare the vinaigrette, mash anchovies with a fork in a small bowl. Whisk vinegar and oil into anchovies until smooth.

Lightly cut a cross on the bottom of the tomatoes (this will make it easier to peel them later). To blanch the tomatoes, place them in salted boiling water for 1 minute. Remove and put immediately into ice water. Peel tomatoes and add the Italian parsley, basil, shallot and vinaigrette. Refrigerate for 10 to 15 minutes before serving. Salt and pepper to taste.

Arugula Salad with Cured Duck Breast

Serves 4

The peppery taste of arugula is just the thing to showcase these slices of cured duck breast. Being from Provence, I especially like the lavender honey in the vinaigrette.

Place the Dijon mustard, vinegar, honey and diced shallot in a small bowl. Season with salt and pepper to taste. Whisk together for 1 minute. Then slowly whisk in olive oil.

Put arugula in a large bowl. Drizzle with the vinaigrette. Mix gently with tongs and serve on salad plates. Place cured duck breast and yellow pepper on top. Sprinkle the salad with sesame seeds. Garnish with chive and chervil sprigs.

VINAIGRETTE:

1   teaspoon Dijon mustard

3   tablespoons champagne vinegar

1   teaspoon lavender honey

1   shallot, diced

¾   cup extra-virgin olive oil

Salt and pepper

SALAD:

6   cups arugula

4   (2-ounce) slices cured duck breast

6   gold baby Peppadew peppers
    (or roasted yellow bell peppers)

1   tablespoon toasted sesame seeds

Chive and chervil sprigs, to garnish

Frisée Salad with Grilled Calamari

Serves 4

VINAIGRETTE:

1½ teaspoons honey

2 tablespoons soy sauce

3 tablespoons extra-virgin olive oil

½ teaspoon garlic puree

1 tablespoon white wine vinegar

1 tablespoon lemon juice

SALAD:

6 calamari tentacles, about 2 ounces each

12 asparagus tips

6 cups frisée

1 teaspoon saffron strands

1 teaspoon black sesame seeds

Along the Mediterranean, we eat a lot of light lunches built around a fresh, crisp salad and some form of protein. Here's one of my favorites that let a touch of Asia gracefully sneak in.

Combine all the vinaigrette ingredients together in a small bowl, mixing well.

Dip the calamari into the vinaigrette and grill for 3 minutes on each side. Cut in half and add to vinaigrette. Grill the asparagus for one minute on each side. Add to vinaigrette. To serve, remove the calamari and asparagus from the dressing and place on top of plated frisée. Sprinkle with saffron strands and black sesame seeds. Drizzle with the vinaigrette.

¼ cup extra-virgin olive oil, plus extra

1 teaspoon chopped fresh oregano

½ teaspoon garlic puree

½ teaspoon kosher salt, plus extra

¼ teaspoon black pepper, plus extra

2 Japanese eggplants, cut in half lengthwise

2 tablespoons tomato coulis *(see recipe p. 186)*

8 slices Parma prosciutto
  (very thin slices, almost transparent)

2 ounces shaved aged Parmesan

4 sprigs oregano, to garnish

Grilled Japanese Eggplant with Prosciutto and Shaved Parmesan

Serves 4

I think grilling is one of the best ways to turn raw eggplant into cooked eggplant. In this case, the wonderful vegetable becomes a kind of instant lasagna.

Preheat the oven to 375° F.

Mix olive oil, ½ teaspoon of the chopped oregano, garlic and the salt and pepper together in a small bowl. Salt and pepper the halved eggplants, and sprinkle the olive oil mixture on top. Place eggplants on the grill and grill for 3 minutes on each side.

Lightly cover with tomato coulis on a sheet pan. Bake for 15 minutes, until tender.

Remove from the oven and lay prosciutto slices on top. Add a layer of Parmesan. Drizzle with olive oil and sprinkle with the remaining chopped oregano. Broil for 5 minutes. Garnish with oregano sprigs and tomato coulis.

CREAMY JASMINE RICE:

2 cups uncooked jasmine rice

2 tablespoons vegetable oil

½ small onion, diced

1 bay leaf

½ teaspoon kosher salt

½ cup heavy cream

SEA BASS:

6 (5-ounce) Chilean sea bass fillets

1 quart water

1 bunch cilantro (leaves only)

2 cups chicken stock (see recipe p. 184)

Salt and pepper

GARNISH:

18 sprigs fresh chives

12 sprigs cilantro

3 teardrop tomatoes, cut in half

Chilean Sea Bass with Creamy Jasmine Rice

Serves 6

One of the most popular fish among restaurant customers these days, the flaky white deliciousness of sea bass is the perfect counterpoint to this creamy, almost-risotto of an aromatic rice.

Preheat the oven to 350° F.

Wash the rice in cold water until the water runs clear. Put oil in a small saucepot, add onion and bay leaf and cook over medium heat until just soft but not caramelized. Add the rice and stir together for 3 minutes. Season with salt. Cook over low heat for 10 to 15 more minutes, stirring occasionally, until rice is tender. Strain in a colander. Spread rice out on a sheet pan to cool. Just before plating, sauté the jasmine rice for 3 to 5 minutes with heavy cream until the cream is completely absorbed.

Salt and pepper sea bass and pan sear both sides for 2 minutes in a sauté pan over low heat, until a nice crust forms. Bake for 6 to 8 minutes, until cooked through.

Blanch cilantro in salted boiling water until bright green, about 5 minutes. Remove from the boiling water and immediately plunge into ice water to maintain the color. Squeeze all the water out. Blend the cilantro with chicken stock in a food processor and pass it through a fine sieve. Season with salt and pepper to taste.

Pour the cilantro broth into a soup bowl, place a spoonful of creamy jasmine rice in the middle and top with sea bass. Garnish with chive sprigs, cilantro and teardrop tomatoes.

FISH:

2   zucchini

2   yellow squash

4   medium tomatoes

4   leeks, white part only

1   lemon, to garnish

4   (16 x 24-inch) sheets of parchment paper

4   (7-ounce) red snapper fillets

SAUCE:

¼   cup vegetable oil

¾   cup extra-virgin olive oil

1   cup sweet white wine

Juice from one lemon

5   tablespoons unsalted butter, melted

3   tablespoons chopped fresh dill

Salt and white pepper

Parchment Paper Red Snapper

Serves 4

Here you have one amazing presentation, sometimes referred to in French as *en papillote,* meaning "in a paper bag." Be sure to keep the parchment satchel sealed until you set it in front of your guests. You (and especially they) will love the aroma when they slice the bag open.

Preheat the oven to 375° F.

Slice zucchini, yellow squash and tomatoes into thin slices. Julienne white parts of leeks. Cut lemon into 5 slices.

Make the sauce by whisking oils, wine and lemon juice together. Gradually whisk butter into the oil mix. Add dill and salt and pepper to taste. Set the sauce aside.

Fold a sheet of parchment paper in half. Open it again. Place a bed of julienned leeks on the half closest to you. Lay a red snapper fillet on top of the leeks. Salt and pepper the top of the fillet. Drizzle some sauce on top of the fillet. Surround the fish with slices of zucchini and yellow squash overlapping each other. Lay out sliced tomatoes overlapping on top of the red snapper fillet. Drizzle more sauce over the whole papillote. Close the parchment paper. Fold edges and crimp together with your fingers. You should have a half moon shape in front of you. Repeat this procedure for the other 3 fillets. Bake for 15 minutes, until parchment is puffed up.

GREEN OIL:

1   bunch Italian parsley

1   bunch basil

3   cups extra-virgin olive oil

FENNEL CONFIT:

6   fennel bulbs, chopped

1   tablespoon extra-virgin olive oil

1   tablespoon unsalted butter

2   tablespoons chopped fresh thyme

Salt and pepper

SEA BASS:

6   (7-ounce) striped bass fillets

1   tablespoon extra-virgin olive oil

12 Roma tomatoes, thinly sliced

¼   cup plus 2 tablespoons balsamic reduction
    (see recipe p. 187)

6   lemon quarters, to garnish

Salt and pepper

Baked Striped Bass with Fennel–Confit Pesto

Serves 6

I'm happy that, with the popularity of Chilean sea bass, more and more diners are opening their minds and their mouths to a previously underutilized fish. Striped bass is beloved along the U.S. Atlantic coast, and needs to be more beloved all over.

Preheat the oven to 350° F.

Blanch the parsley and basil by adding to boiling water for about 1 minute and then immediately plunging into ice water. Squeeze all the water out and chop lightly. Blend all green oil ingredients in a food processor until smooth.

To make the fennel confit, chop the bulbs into ¼-inch pieces and cook in a large saucepan with olive oil, butter and thyme over low heat until tender. Season with salt and pepper to taste.

Season the fish with salt and pepper and sear in a preheated pan with olive oil for 4 minutes on each side. Make a bed of fennel confit on a buttered cast-iron pan. Lay the fish on top of the fennel. Cover the fish with tomato slices, overlapping each other. Season with salt and pepper and bake for 8 minutes, until fish is flaky. Drizzle each fillet with 1 tablespoon each of green oil and balsamic reduction. Garnish each serving with a lemon quarter.

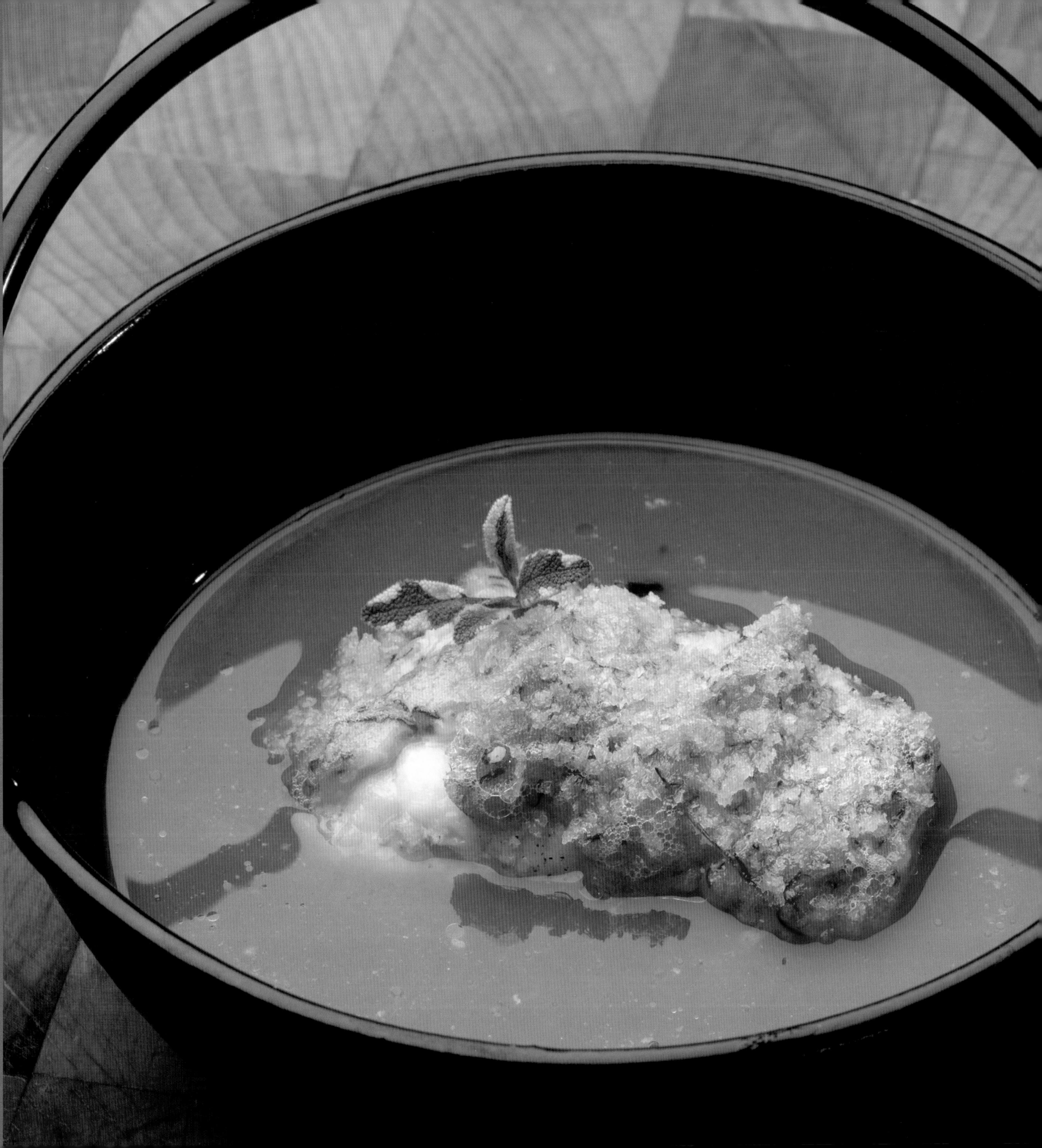

¼ cup extra-virgin olive oil

1 whole fennel head, chopped

1 onion, chopped

1 carrot, chopped

1 leek, chopped

2 (1-pound) red snapper fillets,
   scaled and cleaned

Bones and heads of 2 groupers

2 pounds small crabs or crawfish

½ cup pastis

1 cup dry white wine

1 quart water

1 tablespoon saffron powder

1 (15-ounce) can crushed tomatoes

2 tablespoons tomato paste

2 tablespoons rice

1 tablespoon kosher salt

1 teaspoon black pepper

4 cloves garlic

1 tablespoon chopped fresh thyme

½ cup chopped fresh basil

ROUILLE MAHI MAHI:

Salt and pepper

4 (5-ounce) mahi mahi fillets

½ cup plus 1 tablespoon extra-virgin olive oil

1 fingerling potato, boiled and peeled

1 egg yolk

½ teaspoon garlic puree

1 teaspoon Dijon mustard

1 teaspoon saffron powder

⅓ cup vegetable oil

Crusted Saffron Rouille Mahi Mahi with Marseillaise Soup

Serves 4

This main course is a bit of a fish dish and a bit of a savory soup, all rolled into one. Along the Mediterranean in Provence, we love anything that mixes our fresh local seafood with an intensely flavorful seafood broth.

In a large pot or Dutch oven, heat the olive oil and add fennel, onion, carrot and leek, sautéing until they begin to caramelize. Add all the fish, bones and shellfish; cook together for 10 minutes over medium-high heat. Flambé with pastis, then deglaze with white wine and reduce by about half. Add the remaining soup ingredients and simmer for an hour and a half. Blend everything and pass through a sieve. Keep liquid warm.

Season the mahi mahi with salt and pepper to taste and sear it in a preheated pan with 1 tablespoon olive oil over medium-high heat for 5 minutes on each side. To make the rouille, mash the potato with the egg yolk, garlic, Dijon mustard and saffron in a mixing bowl. Slowly whisk in the vegetable oil and ½ cup olive oil until smooth. Season with salt and pepper to taste.

Ladle the soup into bowls or deep dinner plates. Set the fish in the center. Spoon the rouille over the fish and garnish with fresh basil.

16 large clams

1½ cups sweet white wine

½ cup water

8 fingerling potatoes, thinly sliced

8 ounces fresh Spanish chorizo

¼ cup extra-virgin olive oil

1 teaspoon garlic puree

¼ cup chopped shallots

½ teaspoon salt

⅛ teaspoon black pepper

3 tablespoons tomato coulis *(see recipe p. 186)*

3 tablespoons chopped Italian parsley

1 sprig rosemary, to garnish

Clam Etouffee with Chorizo and Fingerling Potatoes

Serves 4

Here's an idea so good that it works with several different types of shellfish. Clams are a favorite at Le Mistral, but Mediterranean blue mussels are great, too.

In a large sauté pan with a tight lid, steam the clams in white wine and water until they open, about 10 minutes. Pour clams and juice into a large bowl.

Using the same sauté pan, sauté potatoes and chorizo in olive oil over medium heat for 5 minutes. Add garlic puree, shallots and salt and pepper. Cook for another minute and add tomato coulis. Just before serving, transfer clams and juice back to the sauté pan. Cook for 1 more minute. Add parsley. Garnish with rosemary.

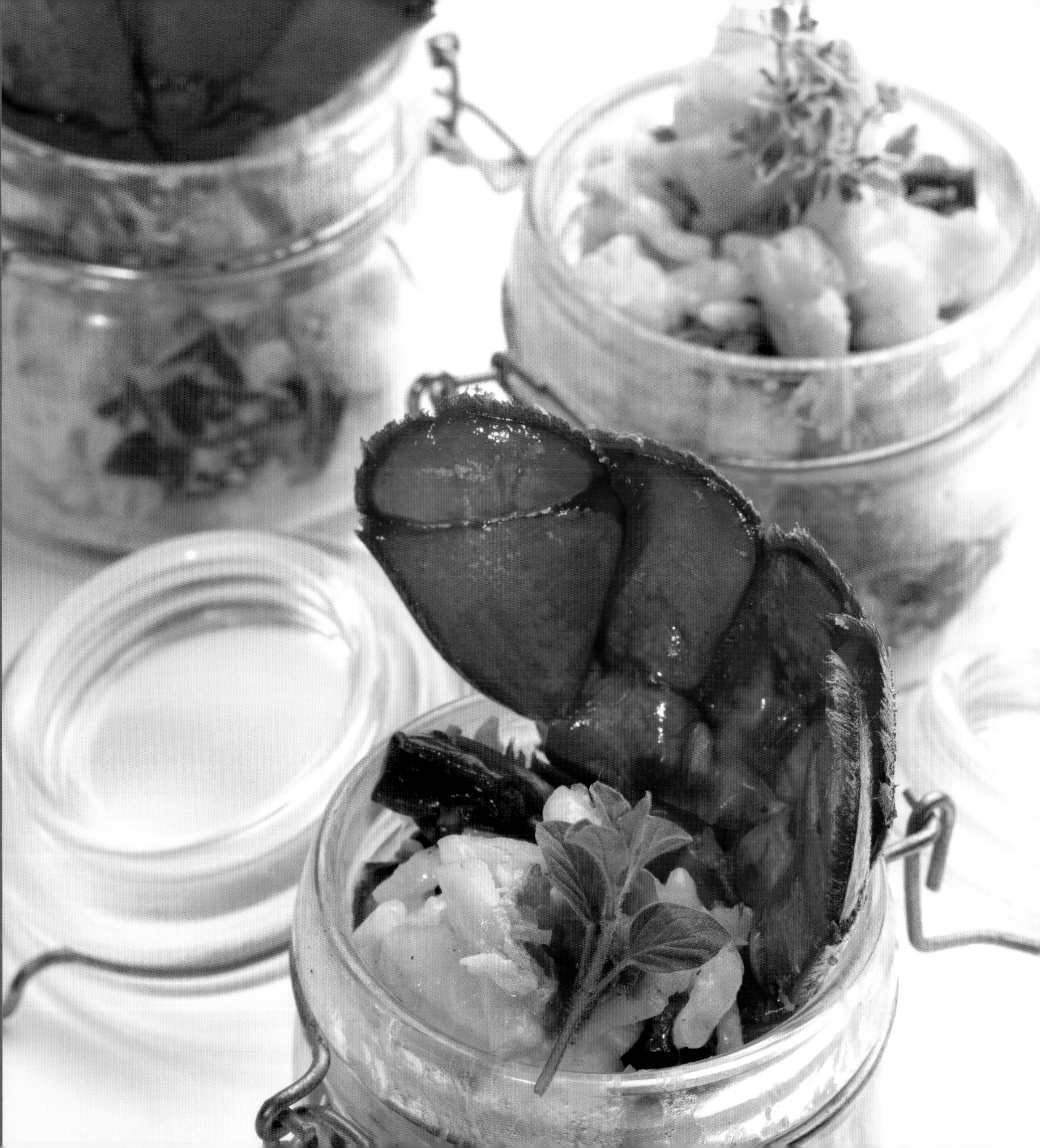

1   white onion, diced

1   tablespoon unsalted butter

3   cups carnaroli or Arborio rice

1   cup white wine

2   cups water

1   cup fish stock or clam juice

12   ounces raw lobster tail

2   tablespoons unsalted butter

Sea salt and white pepper

2   tablespoons finely chopped shallots

½   cup sweet vermouth

4   cups fresh baby spinach

½   cup clam juice

1   cup heavy cream

1   sprig oregano, to garnish

Lobster and Spinach Risotto

Serves 4

Of course plain risotto is always good with anything, or all by itself. If you want to turn it into an impressive lunch or dinner entrée, just add chunks of sweet lobster tail.

To prepare the risotto, sauté onion in butter until lightly caramelized. Add rice and stir until it starts to color, then add white wine, water and fish stock. Cook, stirring often, for 12 minutes and set aside.

Cut lobster in cubes, keeping the tail for decoration. Sauté lobster in 1 tablespoon of the butter. Season to taste with salt and pepper. Add shallots. Flambé with vermouth. Remove from pan. In the same sauté pan, melt 1 tablespoon of butter and sauté the spinach. Add cooked risotto and clam juice. Heat through, 1 to 2 minutes. Add the lobster to the risotto. Add cream and reduce for 5 to 6 minutes. Serve risotto in a large bowl or platter, with the lobster tail for decoration. Garnish with the oregano sprig.

SAUCE:

1   tablespoon unsalted butter

1   onion, diced

½   cup white wine

1   tablespoon chopped fresh tarragon

2   cups chicken stock *(see recipe p. 184)*

½   cup heavy cream

1   tablespoon roux *(see recipe p. 187)*

Salt and pepper

POT PIE:

2   zucchini

2   yellow squash

1   pound white-cap button mushrooms

2   tablespoons vegetable oil

1   teaspoon salt, plus extra

⅛   teaspoon white pepper, plus extra

1   tablespoon chopped fresh tarragon

4   (6-ounce) chicken breasts, cut into strips

1   sheet puff pastry

1   egg yolk, beaten

Zucchini and Squash Chicken Pot Pie

Serves 4

Chicken pot pie is an all–American classic, given just a little French finesse in this recipe. If you like the construction but prefer a different flavor, just build your pot pie with turkey strips, chunks of lobster, clams or mussels.

Preheat the oven to 375° F.

To make the sauce, heat butter in a large sauté pan over medium-high heat. Add onion and cook until caramelized. Deglaze the pan with white wine. Reduce the liquid by half. Add the tarragon, chicken stock and heavy cream, and slowly reduce for 15 to 20 minutes, until thick. Add roux and cook for another 10 to 12 minutes. Salt and pepper to taste.

For the pie, slice zucchini, yellow squash and mushrooms into thin ½-inch slices. Put 1 tablespoon of the oil in a sauté pan, add salt and pepper and sauté all vegetables together until tender. Remove vegetables from the sauté pan, drain the liquid out and set aside.

Put remaining oil in the same sauté pan, add the tarragon and brown the chicken strips until golden. Do not cook through. Season with salt and pepper to taste. Mix vegetables and chicken together in a large bowl.

Cut puff pastry into four 4-inch circles. From the remaining puff pastry, cut 32 strips of puff pastry 4 inches long and ¼ inch wide. Take four ovenproof bowls (3½ inches wide) and spoon the vegetable and chicken mix onto the bottom. Cover with the sauce. Brush the egg yolk around the edges of the bowls. Set a puff pastry circle on top of each bowl. Brush the top of the puff pastry with remaining yolk, and decorate with pastry strips. Bake for 12 to 14 minutes, until golden and puffy.

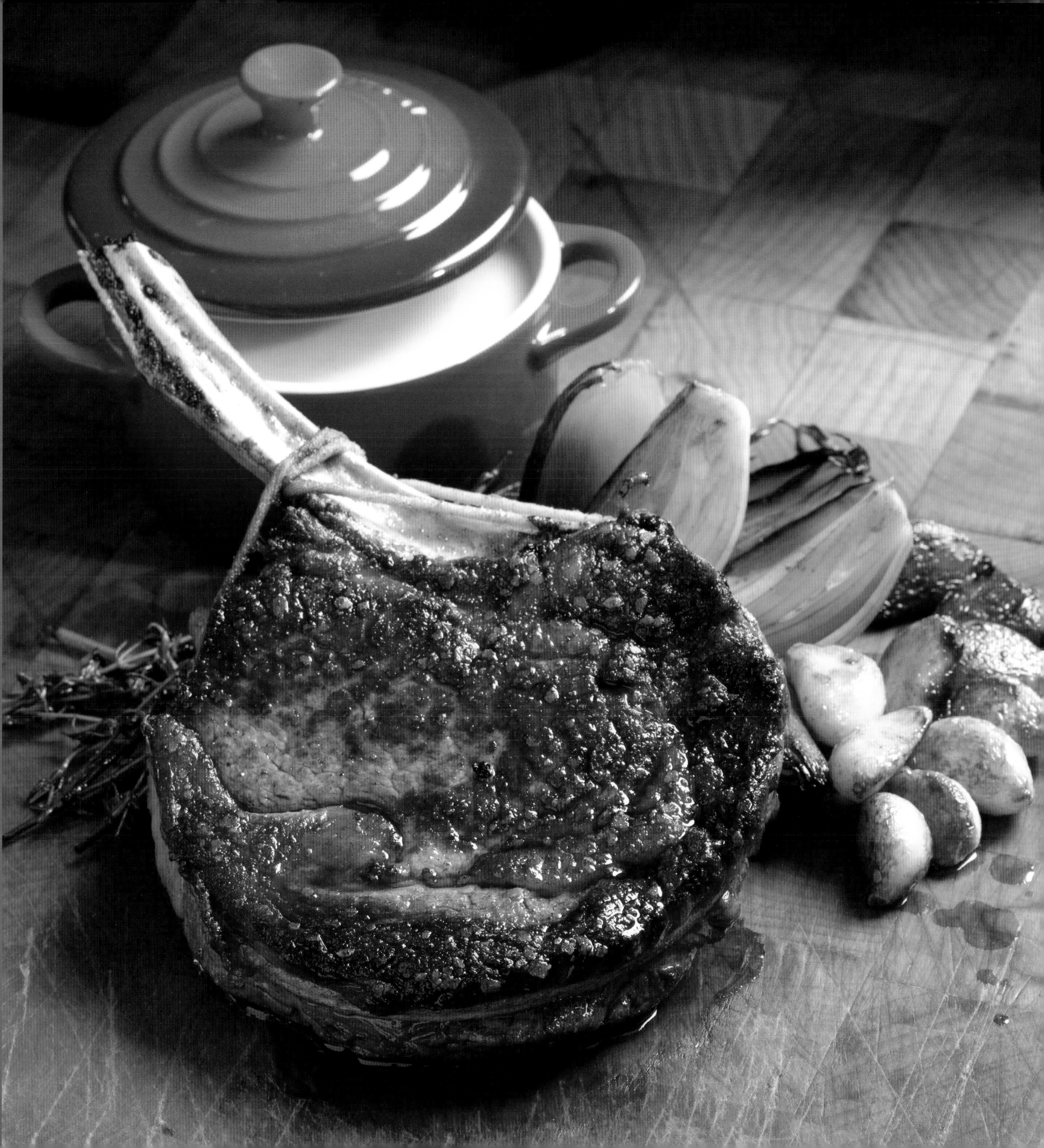

4 cups peeled and diced Idaho baking potatoes

¾ cup whole milk

1 teaspoon salt, plus extra

¼ teaspoon white pepper, plus extra

¾ cup heavy cream

1 stick unsalted butter

STEAK:

4 tablespoons (½ stick) butter

8 shallots, quartered

20 cloves garlic

12 sprigs thyme

8 sprigs sage

½ teaspoon kosher salt, plus extra

½ teaspoon freshly ground black pepper,
   plus extra

4 (10-ounce) dry-aged, bone-in rib-eye steaks

Dry-Aged Cowboy Steak with Pomme Mousseline

Serves 4

You can't be a success as a restaurant in Texas unless you can be a success with steak. I think you'll find that this recipe takes "meat and potatoes" to a whole new level.

Preheat the oven to 375° F.

Put all pomme mousseline ingredients except butter into a large saucepan. Cook over low heat until potatoes are soft, about 30 minutes. Drain potatoes and reserve the cooking liquid. Pass potatoes through a fine sieve. Place potatoes in a bowl, add butter and cooking liquid. Season with salt and pepper to taste and mix slowly together.

To prepare the steak, heat 2 tablespoons of the butter in an ovenproof skillet over medium-high heat. Add shallots, garlic, thyme, sage, salt and pepper, cooking until caramelized. Remove from the skillet.

Salt and pepper the steaks on both sides. In the skillet over high heat, sear the steak in the remaining butter for 2 minutes on each side. Place the steak in the skillet in the oven and bake until the meat reaches medium rare, 8 to 10 minutes. Garnish steak with shallot mixture. Serve the pomme mousseline on the side.

CANDIED VEGETABLES:

4 baby carrots

2 baby red beets

6 baby turnips

1 tablespoon honey

1½ cups water

½ tablespoon unsalted butter

Salt and pepper

LAMB:

1 (8-chop) rack of Australian lamb (ask butcher
   to clean and "French" the lamb)

3 tablespoons unsalted butter

3 whole peeled shallots

2 sprigs fresh rosemary

2 sprigs fresh thyme

2 cloves garlic

Salt and pepper

SAUCE:

½ carrot, diced

3 black peppercorns

¼ cinnamon stick

1 tablespoon powdered ginger

2 tablespoons honey

1 clove

1 bay leaf

¼ cup dry white wine

1 quart lamb stock (see recipe p. 185)

Salt and pepper

Rack of Lamb with Ginger Sauce and Candied Baby Vegetables

Serves 2

It's tough to decide if this dramatic slow-roasted lamb dish looks better than it tastes, or tastes even better than it looks.

Preheat the oven to 375° F.

To make the candied vegetables, peel all the vegetables and place in a large soup or sauce pot with all ingredients except butter, salt and pepper. Cook over medium-high heat until water is completely evaporated, starting to give a glaze to the vegetables. Then add the butter. Season to taste with salt and pepper. Keep warm.

Salt and pepper the rack of lamb. Brown it in a large sauté pan with about half the butter. Remove from the pan. In the same pan, using the remaining butter, sauté the shallots, rosemary, thyme and garlic until lightly caramelized. Spread this mixture on a sheet pan and set rack of lamb on top. Roast it in the preheated oven for 18 to 20 minutes. Let the lamb rest wrapped in aluminum foil for 10 minutes before slicing.

To prepare the sauce, transfer vegetables from the sheet pan into a large saucepan. Cook them over medium-high heat with the carrot, black peppercorns, cinnamon stick, ginger powder, honey, clove and bay leaf until golden brown. Pour in the wine and reduce by half. Add the lamb stock and reduce by three quarters. Season to taste with salt and pepper.

To serve, carve rack into 8 chops. Place on a platter, with candied vegetables spread around and sauce drizzled over the top.

4 fingerling potatoes, cut in half lengthwise

2 yellow tomatoes, tops removed and reserved

2 baby zucchini, cut in half lengthwise

1 eggplant, cut in half lengthwise

2 small sweet onions

½ French baguette, sliced

2 cups whole milk

4 cloves garlic

1 bunch Italian parsley

½ pound cooked ham

½ cup chopped onion

Salt and pepper

¼ cup Japanese (Panko) bread crumbs

3 tablespoons extra-virgin olive oil

Stuffed Baby Vegetables

Serves 6

In my region of France, this basic, home-cooking idea is often called *farcis de Provence,* which we might translate with a smile as "stuffed stuff from Provence."

Preheat the oven to 375° F.

Gently remove the inside of each vegetable with a paring knife and set the shells and the insides aside. Soak the bread in bowl of milk until soft, about 10 minutes. Remove bread and squeeze out the liquid. Put insides of hollowed vegetables, the soaked baguette, garlic, parsley, ham and chopped onion in a food processor. Grind until fine.

Salt and pepper the insides of the vegetable shells. Fill each of the shells with the stuffing. Sprinkle the top of the stuffed vegetables with Panko bread crumbs. Drizzle with olive oil. Bake in the oven for 40 minutes, until golden brown.

ROSEMARY VEAL SAUCE:

½ tablespoon butter

2 shallots, thinly sliced

2 cups aged Port wine

1 cup veal demi-glace *(see recipe p. 186)*

¼ teaspoon chopped fresh rosemary

Salt and pepper

FRICASSEE:

2 king trumpet mushrooms, thinly sliced

1 cup chanterelle mushrooms, quartered

1 cup velvet pioppini mushrooms

1 cup black trumpet mushrooms, halved

1 cup white enoki mushrooms

1 tablespoon butter

1½ teaspoons garlic puree

½ teaspoon chopped fresh thyme

2 teaspoons chopped fresh Italian parsley

2 tablespoons chopped shallot

Oregano and sage sprigs, to garnish

Wild Mushroom Fricassee

Serves 4

For lovers of fresh mushrooms, this side dish is a festival. And I think you'll love the flavors delivered by the rosemary veal sauce.

To make the sauce, melt butter in a sauté pan over medium-high heat. Add shallots and cook until golden brown. Deglaze the pan with the Port wine and cook until liquid is reduced by half. Add veal demi-glace and rosemary, and slowly reduce for about 20 minutes. Pass sauce through a fine sieve. Season with salt and pepper to taste. Keep sauce warm.

Clean mushrooms with a dry towel (do not wash or put the mushrooms in water). Heat butter in a sauté pan over low heat. When your butter reaches a brown color, add all mushrooms at the same time and slowly sauté for 10 to 12 minutes. (For the first 5 to 6 minutes, water will be released from the mushrooms. For the second 5 to 6 minutes, the water will evaporate and the mushrooms will start to brown.) Add garlic puree, thyme, parsley and shallot. Sauté for another 2 to 3 minutes.

Place the mushroom fricassee in the middle of a plate and surround with the sauce. Garnish each serving with sage leaves and a sprig of oregano.

NAPOLEON:

4 (2½-inch) circles puff pastry

1 egg yolk, lightly beaten

4 (2½-inch by ½-inch) slices Bucheron
   goat cheese

⅛ teaspoon pepper

2 teaspoons honey

Thyme sprigs, to garnish

TOMATO CONFIT:

4 Roma tomatoes

¼ extra-virgin olive oil

1 teaspoon chopped fresh thyme

½ teaspoon minced garlic

½ teaspoon sea salt

⅛ teaspoon white pepper

BASIL PESTO:

4 ounces fresh basil

½ cup extra-virgin olive oil

½ teaspoon minced garlic

1 cup chopped Italian parsley

½ teaspoon kosher salt

⅛ teaspoon white pepper

Bucheron Goat Cheese–Tomato Confit Napoleon

Serves 4

Bucheron is a lovely goat cheese from the Loire Valley. Fairly mild and soft when young, it turns up in stores as a kind of log that can be easily sliced—and, in this case, used as a layer in wonderful vegetable napoleon. And you thought chocolate had all the fun!

Preheat the oven to 300° F.

Lay out the pastry circles on a sheet pan, brush the top with the egg yolk and bake until puffy and golden, 15 to 20 minutes. Remove from the oven and let cool to room temperature.

Pepper the slices of goat cheese and cover them with honey.

To prepare the tomato confit, bring water to a boil in a large pot. Make a cross with a paring knife on the bottom of the tomatoes and add them to the water for about 3 minutes. Remove them and immediately plunge into a bowl of ice water. Remove the skin of the tomatoes. Cut each tomato into quarters and remove the whole inside. This produces 16 tomato quarters, peeled and seeded. Place tomatoes on a sheet pan.

In a small bowl, mix olive oil, thyme, garlic, sea salt and pepper together, then brush tomatoes with this mixture. Cover tomatoes with parchment paper and bake for 15 to 20 minutes. Let the tomatoes cool to room temperature.

To prepare the basil pesto, bring a large pot of water to a boil. Drop basil into the water for 20 seconds and quickly remove it, immediately plunging into a bowl of ice water to keep the green color of the basil. Remove basil from the chilled water and squeeze the extra water out. Chop the leaves and transfer them to a blender or food processor. Add the olive oil, garlic, parsley, kosher salt and white pepper. Blend at low speed just until smooth, 1 to 2 minutes.

To serve, place the tomato confit and slices of goat cheese in the oven for about 5 minutes to warm everything up. Take one puff pastry circle and lay one slice of goat cheese on top. Cover the goat cheese with the tomato confit, then repeat the sequence one more time. Follow the same procedure with the remaining 3 napoleons. Place the napoleons in the middle of appetizer plates with a thyme sprig on top to garnish and a spoonful of basil pesto on the side.

ORANGE MARMALADE:

7 oranges, peeled and segmented

1 cup sugar

2 tablespoons Grand Marnier

1 tablespoon butter

ORANGE SAUCE:

½ cup sugar

1 cup freshly squeezed orange juice

2 tablespoons Grand Marnier

CREPES:

6 eggs

1 tablespoon plus 2 teaspoons all-purpose flour

1 tablespoon plus 2 teaspoons sugar

½ teaspoon vanilla extract

Zest of 1 orange

1 stick unsalted butter, melted

Salt

2 cups whole milk

1 tablespoon Grand Marnier

Traditional Crepes Suzette

Serves 4

In a French restaurant, it's hard to imagine any dessert more elegant that crepes suzette flamed tableside. At home, you can enjoy everything about this grand old dessert—without even wearing a head waiter's tuxedo.

To prepare the marmalade, cook oranges and sugar over low heat for 1 hour. Let cool. Gently stir in Grand Marnier, followed by the butter.

To prepare the sauce, carefully melt the sugar in a saucepan over low heat. Pour in the orange juice and bring the mixture to a boil. Reduce for 20 minutes over low heat. Let cool. Stir in Grand Marnier.

Whisk eggs, flour, sugar, vanilla, orange zest, melted butter and a pinch of salt together, until completely smooth. Slowly whisk in the milk. Let batter rest in the refrigerator for 2 to 4 hours, until smooth and incorporated. Preheat a crepe pan and butter it. Pour a light coating of batter into the pan and cook for just 1 minute per side, flipping the crepe with your hands and a flick of the wrist or with the help of a spatula. Let cool.

To serve, preheat and butter a cast iron pan. Fold cooled crepes into a half-moon shape. Spoon 1 tablespoon orange marmalade onto the crepe and fold in half again; you should have a triangle. Place the crepe into the pan and warm for 2 minutes per side. Carefully add the 1 tablespoon Grand Marnier and flambé. Spoon sauce around the crepes and serve immediately.

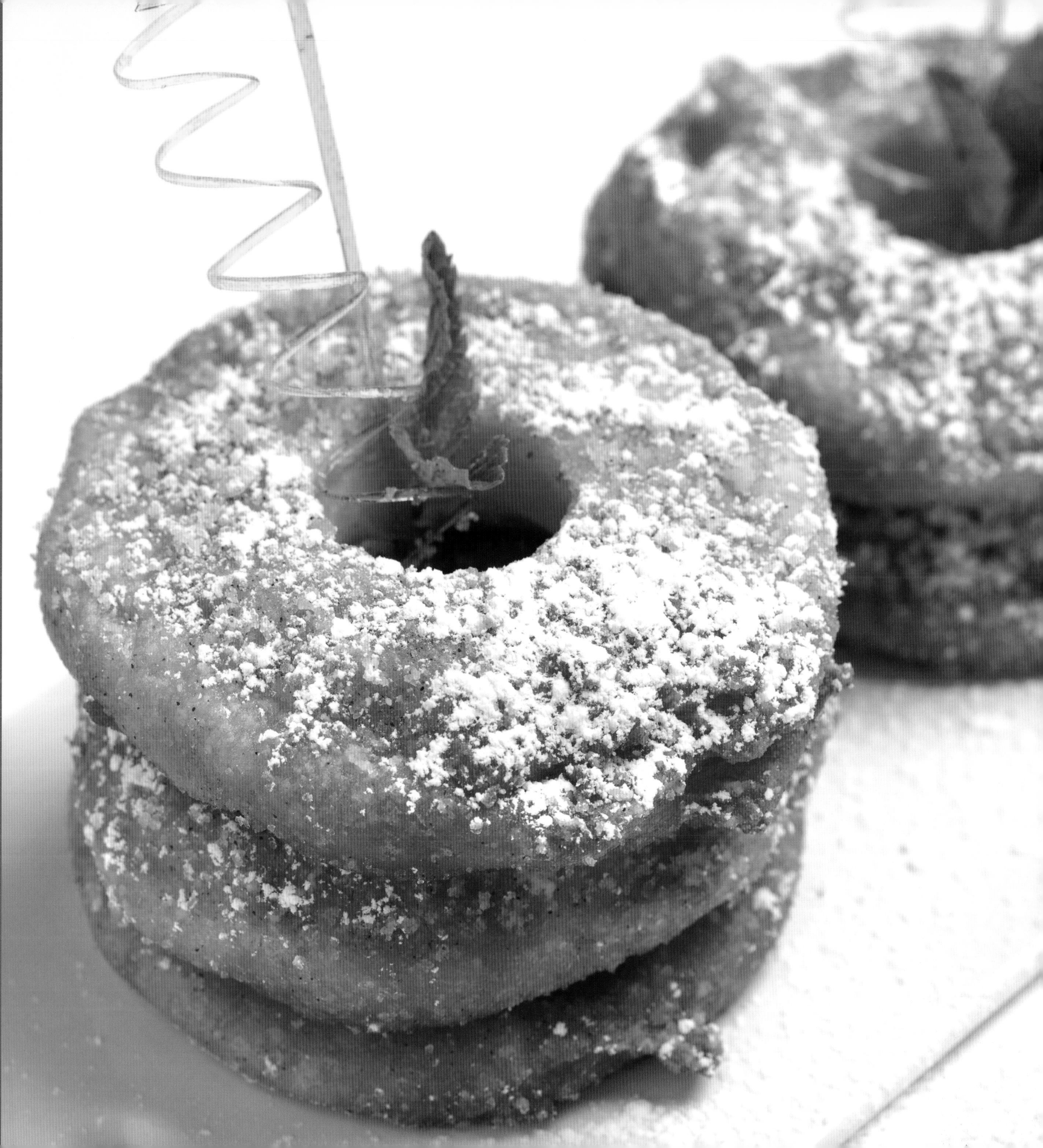

½ cup all-purpose flour

¼ cup sugar

2 egg yolks

1 teaspoon vanilla extract

¾ cup beer

½ cup whole milk

4 egg whites

2 golden apples

1 quart vegetable oil, for deep-frying

Powdered sugar

Fresh mint, for garnish

Beignets aux Pommes de Meme Poucel

Serves 4

Beignets are light, usually airy doughnuts, as visitors to the New Orleans French Quarter tend to know well. In traditional French cooking, however, they are also fritters filled with sweet ripe fruit. Apples always make me think of Normandy.

In a large bowl, whisk together flour, sugar, egg yolks, vanilla extract and beer. Slowly whisk in the milk.

In a separate bowl, beat the egg whites with a pinch of salt, until fluffy. Slowly fold egg whites into the flour mixture.

Peel and core the apples and slice them sideways into rings. Then dip them once and then again into the batter mixture. Fry these beignets for 3 to 4 minutes in vegetable oil over medium-high heat. Sprinkle with powdered sugar. Garnish with mint.

GRATINÉE:

12 (6-inch) pieces red rhubarb

1   cup sugar

2   cups water

1   bay leaf

5   black peppercorns

3   tablespoons unsalted butter

Fresh mint, to garnish

WHIPPED CREAM:

1   cup heavy cream

2   tablespoons powdered sugar

¼   teaspoon vanilla extract

Rhubarb Gratinée

Serves 4

Like any other dessert involving rhubarb, this one is also excellent when bright red strawberries are added to the mix. The gratinée delivers a delightful crunch on top.

Slowly simmer rhubarb, sugar, water, bay leaf and peppercorns in a saucepan until soft, about 8 minutes. Gently remove the rhubarb from the syrup. Reduce remaining liquid over high heat until syrupy and whisk in the butter. Strain through a fine sieve.

Using a whisk in a chilled stainless steel bowl, whip the cream with the sugar and vanilla until fluffy. (Do not overbeat the cream or it will become butter.) Refrigerate until ready to serve.

Place the rhubarb in individual ramekins and top with syrup. Put ramekin under a preheated broiler for 4 to 5 minutes, until the top is golden brown. Spoon the whipped cream on top. Garnish with mint.

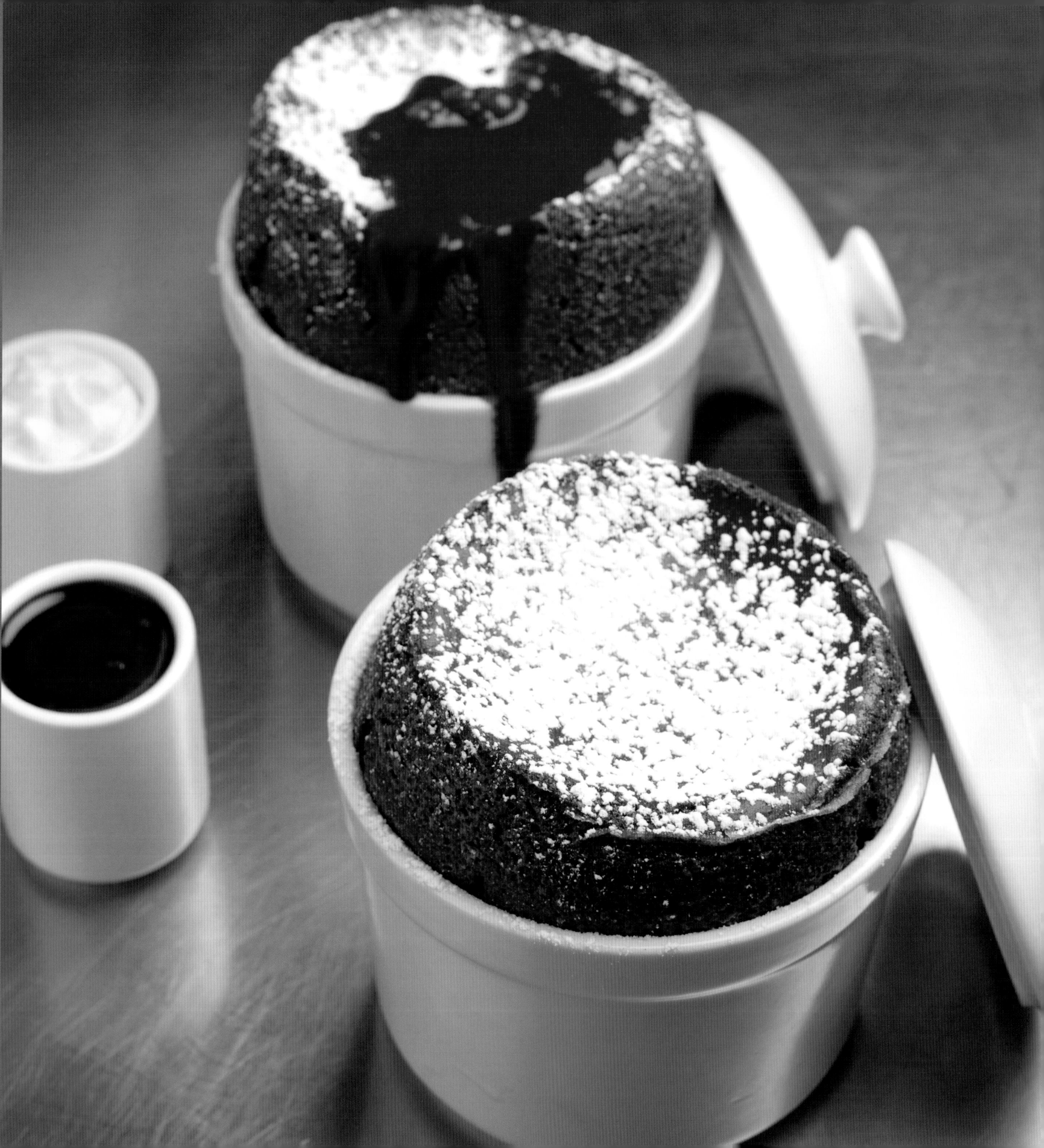

Le Mistral Chocolate Soufflé

Serves 6

Being a French restaurant, Le Mistral is naturally considered a destination for chocolate soufflé. Making these things isn't as hard as some people think, though it is essential they be served right away—while they're still puffed up with hot air from the oven.

Preheat the oven to 375° F.

Butter 6 individual soufflé ramekins and sprinkle with sugar; set aside.

Melt chocolate in a metal bowl over barely simmering water, stirring constantly. Once the chocolate is melted, remove the bowl from heat and stir in the egg yolks.

In a separate bowl, beat egg whites with salt on medium-high speed until they hold soft glossy peaks. Continue beating egg whites on high speed, gradually adding the remaining ⅓ cup sugar, until the egg whites hold stiff glossy peaks.

Gently stir ⅓ of the eggs whites into the chocolate mixture, then carefully fold in the remaining egg whites. The chocolate mixture should be light and bubbly, and even-colored without egg-white streaks.

Spoon the soufflé mixture into the prepared ramekins and bake for 13 to 16 minutes, until puffed up and golden brown.

While the soufflés are baking, prepare the chocolate sauce. Warm the cream, then stir in the chocolate chips until melted and thoroughly incorporated.

Serve soufflés with a dusting of powdered sugar if desired and the chocolate sauce on the side.

SOUFFLÉ:

Unsalted butter

⅓ cup granulated sugar, plus 2 tablespoons for sprinkling

5 ounces good-quality dark chocolate, broken into pieces

3 egg yolks, at room temperature

6 egg whites, at room temperature

¹⁄₁₆ teaspoon salt

Powdered sugar, optional

CHOCOLATE SAUCE:

3 cups heavy cream

18 ounces semi-sweet chocolate chips

COULIS:

½ cup water

½ cup sugar

½ sprig fresh rosemary

3 cups fresh raspberries

ROSEMARY WHIPPED CREAM:

2 cups heavy whipping cream

½ teaspoon ground rosemary

½ cup powdered sugar

½ teaspoon vanilla extract

36 fresh raspberries

Fresh Raspberries with Raspberry Coulis and Rosemary Whipped Cream

Serves 6

When raspberries are in season, there's really nothing better. This mix of fresh berries and a nice coulis is even more interesting when paired with the whipped cream scented with rosemary.

Prepare the coulis by putting water, sugar and rosemary in a saucepan. Then add the raspberries. Let them cook for 10 minutes over low heat. Remove rosemary. Pour the raspberry mixture into a blender and blend until extremely fine. Pass the blended mixture through a sieve to remove the seeds.

Place the cream and ground rosemary in a saucepan and warm over low heat, being careful to not boil the cream. Remove from heat and let sit for 20 minutes. Place the cream in the refrigerator until completely chilled, at least 30 minutes. Add sugar and vanilla to cream and whisk until fluffy. Do not overbeat; it will turn into butter.

To serve, spoon coulis onto the bottom of a dish. Set 6 raspberries on each dish, topped with whipped cream.

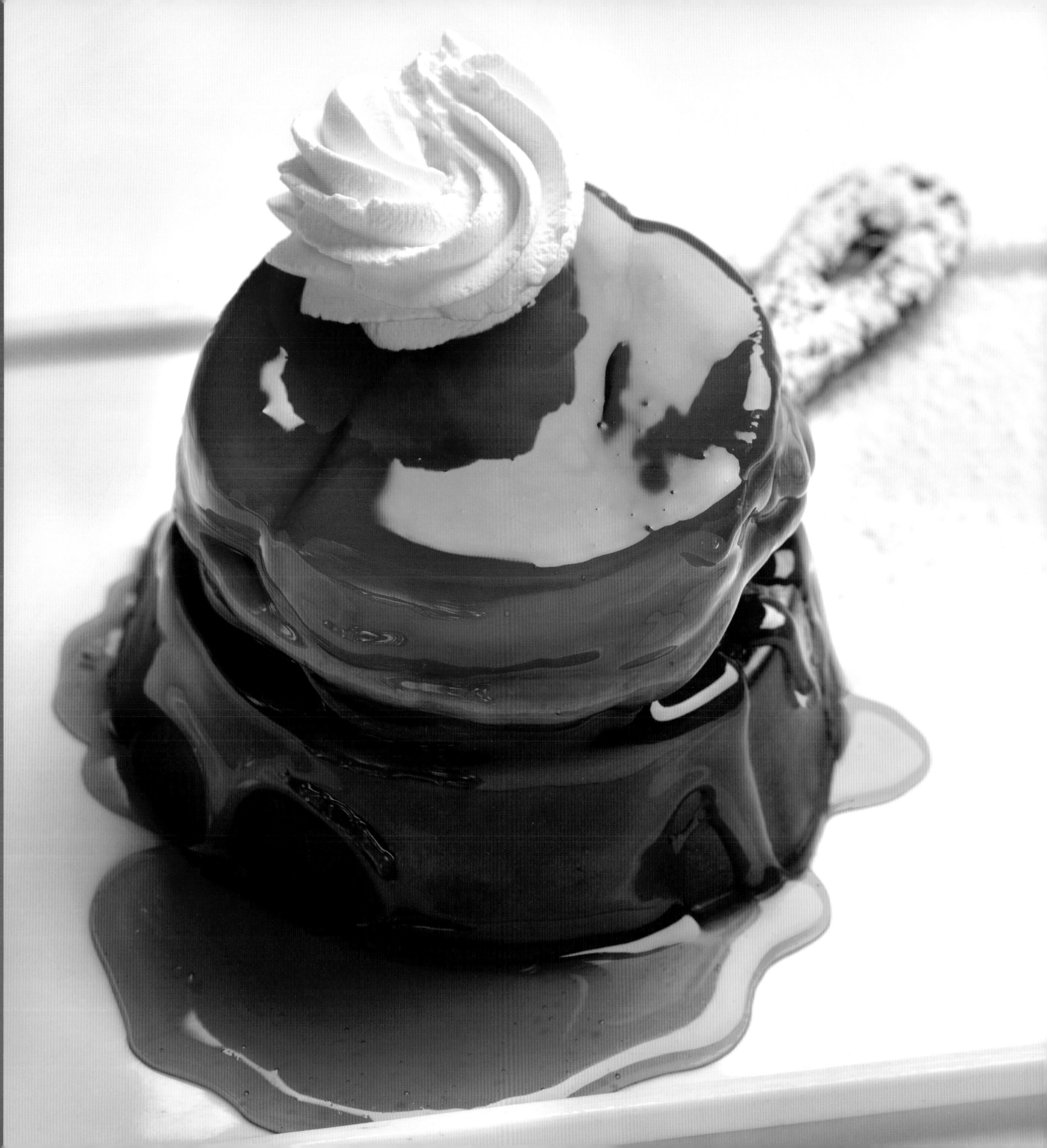

¼ cup plus 2 tablespoons sugar

4 tablespoons (½ stick) unsalted butter

1 sheet puff pastry

4 golden apples

Vanilla ice cream or crème fraîche

Individual Tart Tatins

Serves 4

This is a traditional dessert from the Normandy region of France, where apple trees are everywhere and most people love to drink the apple brandy called Calvados. Calvados, in fact, goes quite nicely with this individual-serving version of this family-style classic.

Preheat the oven to 350° F.

Melt the sugar slowly in a sauté pan over low heat. Do not stir, simply move the pan around gently. Once the sugar reaches a nice caramel color, remove the pan from the heat and slowly stir in the butter. Pour this caramel sauce into individual 4-inch wide molds.

Cut puff pastry into four 4½-inch circles. Peel and core the apples. Cut them into quarters. Divide the apple over the caramel in the molds. Top with a pastry circle and bake until golden brown, 20 to 25 minutes.

Flip from the molds onto dessert plates, so the pastry is on the bottom. Place 1 scoop of vanilla ice cream or crème fraîche on top of the tart. Serve warm.

Bucco Recipes

1½ pounds veal tenderloin or steak

1 tablespoon extra-virgin olive oil

1 tablespoon unsalted butter

Salt and white pepper

TONNATO SAUCE:

2 tablespoons capers

4 anchovy fillets

½ cup extra-virgin olive oil

1 cup canned tuna in oil

2 cups mayonnaise

PARSLEY OIL:

1 cup chopped fresh Italian parsley

½ teaspoon salt

½ cup vegetable oil

Vitello Tonnato

Serves 6

This appetizer is one of our cornerstones at Bucco. It has been on our menu from day one, and you will be hooked from the first bite. That's a promise!

Preheat the oven to 250° F.

Sear the veal lightly on both sides in a sauté pan with the olive oil and butter. Season with salt and white pepper. Place the meat on a sheet pan and bake until the temperature of the meat reaches 125° F. Remove the meat from the oven and let cool. Cut thin slices with a knife or slicing machine.

To make the sauce, put capers, anchovies and olive oil in a food processor and mix well. Add tuna and mayonnaise, and mix until the sauce is smooth.

Remove sauce and clean the processor bowl. Then put in the parsley, salt and oil, and blend for 1 to 2 minutes, until the oil is green and smooth.

Divide the veal slices onto appetizer plates and decorate with spoonfuls of tonnato sauce and parsley oil.

Seared Scallops with Foie Gras and Crawfish Reduction

Serves 4

I love scallops. After my first visit to Houston, I got hooked on cooking big scallops every time I visit. This is my favorite scallop dish.

Start by reducing crawfish stock by half. Season with pastis, salt and pepper. Whisk the butter into the reduction so you will have a thickened, syrupy emulsion sauce.

In a saucepan over low heat, combine shallot, pine nuts, olive oil and salt and pepper to taste. Simmer until shallots are transparent, about 15 minutes.

Sear the scallops in a sauté pan with olive oil and butter, about 1 minute per side. Season with salt and white pepper to taste.

Sear the foie gras slices on a very hot, dry sauté pan about 20 to 30 seconds per side. Season with salt. Just before serving, reheat shallot mixture and add spinach, stirring for 30 seconds.

Serve 2 scallops per person atop a mound of spinach-shallot mixture. Drizzle with the crawfish reduction. Serve immediately.

CRAWFISH REDUCTION:

1   cup crawfish stock (*see recipe p. 185*)
1   tablespoon pastis
1   stick unsalted butter
Salt and white pepper

SAUCE:

1   shallot, thinly sliced
2   tablespoons pine nuts, toasted
½   cup extra virgin olive oil
2   cups fresh baby spinach
Salt and black pepper

SCALLOPS:

8   large sea scallops
1   tablespoon extra-virgin olive oil
1   tablespoon unsalted butter
4   (1-inch-thick) slices of grade A foie gras
Salt and white pepper

BEURRE BLANC:

3 shallots, finely chopped

12 white peppercorns

1 bay leaf

1 tablespoon fresh thyme

¼ cup white wine vinegar

1 cup white wine

1 cup heavy cream

1 stick unsalted butter

Salt and white pepper

ASPARAGUS:

24 stalks green or white asparagus

Salt and pepper

8 thin slices prosciutto

4 tablespoons (½ stick) unsalted butter

¼ cup olive oil

½ cup grated parmigiano

Asparagus Tips Wrapped in Prosciutto with Beurre Blanc

Serves 4

The saltiness of the paper-thin prosciutto offers a delicate but unforgettable counterpart to the tender tips of asparagus.

Preheat the oven to 375° F.

Prepare the beurre blanc. Put the shallots, peppercorns, bay leaf and thyme in a saucepan over high heat. Immediately add the vinegar. Cook for 2 minutes before adding the white wine. Reduce liquid by half. Add the cream and reduce over high heat for about 10 minutes. Strain the sauce into a bowl, then pour it back into the pan. Whisk in the butter. Season with salt and white pepper to taste.

Peel the asparagus from halfway back from the tip. Cut ½ inch off from the stem after peeling. Blanch the asparagus in boiling water for 2 minutes, then plunge immediately into ice water. Drain the asparagus, and salt and pepper to taste.

Lay out the slices of prosciutto side by side. Top each slice with a small piece of butter. Then with 6 asparagus tips in a row, roll the prosciutto around the asparagus. Set the rolls on a sheet pan, pour olive oil on top and sprinkle with grated parmigiano cheese. Bake for 8 to 10 minutes. Serve hot, 2 per person, drizzled with beurre blanc.

CARPACCIO OF ROASTED BEETS:

2 pounds fresh beets, skin on

1 pound rock salt

1 shallot, finely chopped

½ cup balsamic vinegar

1 cup olive oil

1 tablespoon sugar

2 teaspoons salt

½ teaspoon black pepper

SALMON TARTARE:

1 pound cold-smoked salmon fillet

2 tablespoons olive oil

2 tablespoons finely chopped chives

½ teaspoon black pepper

¼ cup fish roe

GOAT CHEESE PASTE:

8 ounces fresh goat cheese

1 tablespoon finely chopped thyme

1 teaspoon honey

½ cup crème fraîche

⅛ teaspoon salt

¼ teaspoon black pepper

1 tablespoon pine nuts, toasted

Cold-Smoked Salmon Tartare with Carpaccio of Roasted Beets

Serves 4 to 6

In Finland, we take our fish-smoking seriously. In this case, the cold smoking delivers a milder taste than hot smoking would, thus letting the salmon itself be the main flavor in this tartare.

Preheat the oven to 350° F.

Place beets on a bed of rock salt on a sheet pan and bake in the oven for 50 to 60 minutes, until they are easily pierced with a fork. Let cool and peel. Cut very thin slices with a knife or slicing machine.

Make the vinegar marinade. Mix shallot, vinegar, oil, sugar, salt and black pepper in a large bowl. Marinate beet slices in this liquid for at least 1 hour.

Dice salmon, and mix with olive oil, chives and black pepper in a large bowl. Using 3-inch-wide ring molds, form salmon into a bottom layer and spoon a teaspoon of fish eggs on top of the tartare.

Peel the skin from goat cheese. Mix all paste ingredients except pine nuts with a fork.

Place beet slices as a thin layer on a plate. Top with tartare. Put goat cheese paste on top of tartare. Sprinkle some toasted pine nuts on top of the cheese.

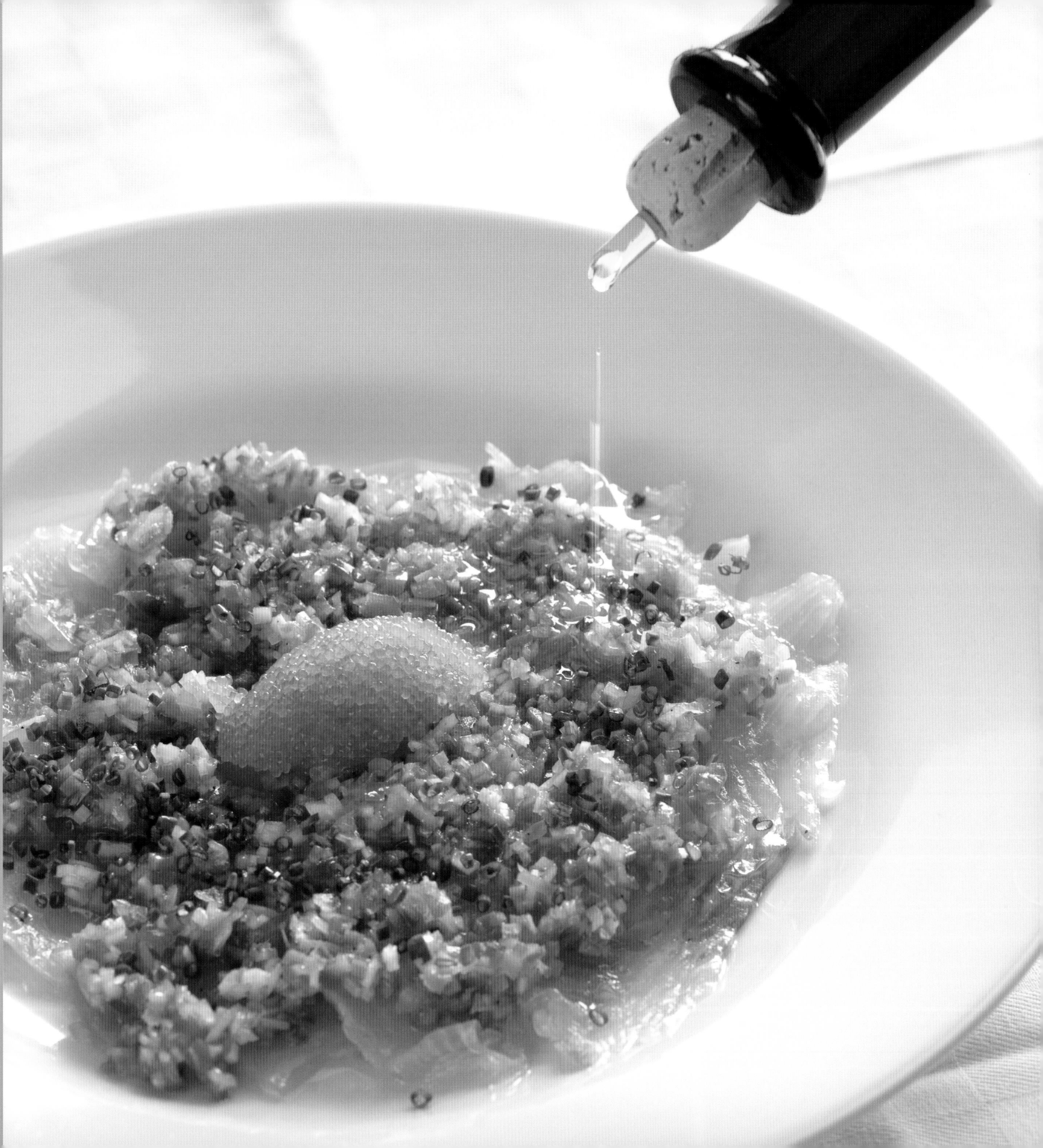

FISH:

1¼ pounds whitefish fillet

¼ cup rock salt

2 tablespoons sugar

SALAD:

½ cup finely chopped green bell pepper

½ cup finely chopped carrots

½ cup finely chopped shallots

½ cup finely chopped fennel (bulb only)

2 tablespoons lemon juice

2 tablespoons finely chopped chives

1 cup olive oil

Salt and black pepper

2 tablespoons fish roe

Coregone Catalunya

Serves 4 to 6

At Bucco, we call whitefish by its Italian name, coregone. But you can make this dish using any white-fleshed, mild-tasting fish fresh from waters near you. The presentation with this colorful salad is inspired by the Basque piperades found along the French-Spanish border in Catalunya.

Lay the fish on a sheet pan and cover on both sides with salt and sugar. Cover the pan with plastic wrap and set in the refrigerator overnight to cure the fish.

Prepare mosaic salad by mixing all the chopped vegetables in a large bowl. Add lemon juice, chives, olive oil and salt and black pepper to taste. Let salad marinate for one hour before serving.

When ready to serve, cut the fish in thin slices and place them on a plate or tray. Top the slices with the salad.

SWEETBREADS:

1¾ pounds veal sweetbreads

1 cup chopped shallots

3 bay leaves

1 tablespoon white peppercorns

1 tablespoon rock salt

Unsalted butter

Salt and white pepper

CARROT JUICE REDUCTION:

2 cups carrot juice

½ cup orange juice

1 tablespoon sugar

1 tablespoon salt

3 tablespoons unsalted butter

2-3 carrots, cut in 4-inch pieces and
    cooked just until tender

MOREL-MARSALA SAUCE:

1 cup coarsely chopped morel mushrooms

1 cup Marsala wine

2 cups veal demi-glace *(see recipe p. 186)*

Salt and pepper

Toasted pistachios (optional)

Sweetbreads with Morel-Marsala Sauce

Serves 4 to 6

If you like sweetbreads—and many people do once they actually get around to trying them—then you'll love what happens to them when wrapped in a warm blanket of marsala sauce with morels.

Start by blanching the sweetbreads. Then replace water from blanching with fresh cold water, keeping sweetbreads in the pot. Add shallots, bay leaves, white peppercorns and rock salt. Bring to a boil and let simmer for two hours. Let sweetbreads cool down in liquid overnight in the refrigerator.

Remove the transparent skin from the sweetbreads using a paring knife and cut into ½-inch-thick slices. Sear slices in a sauté pan with butter over high heat. Season with salt and white pepper to taste.

To prepare carrot juice reduction, put juices, sugar and salt in a saucepan over high heat, until liquid is reduced by half, about 8 minutes. Whisk the butter into the reduction. Add the pieces of precooked carrots.

To make the morel-marsala sauce, soak the mushrooms in Marsala wine for 30 minutes. After soaking, cook mushrooms with Marsala over medium-high heat, until liquid is reduced by half. Add the demi-glace and reduce by half again. Season with salt and pepper to taste.

To serve, place carrots in the center of the plate and top with seared sweetbread slices. Spoon sauce over the mound. If desired, decorate with toasted pistachios.

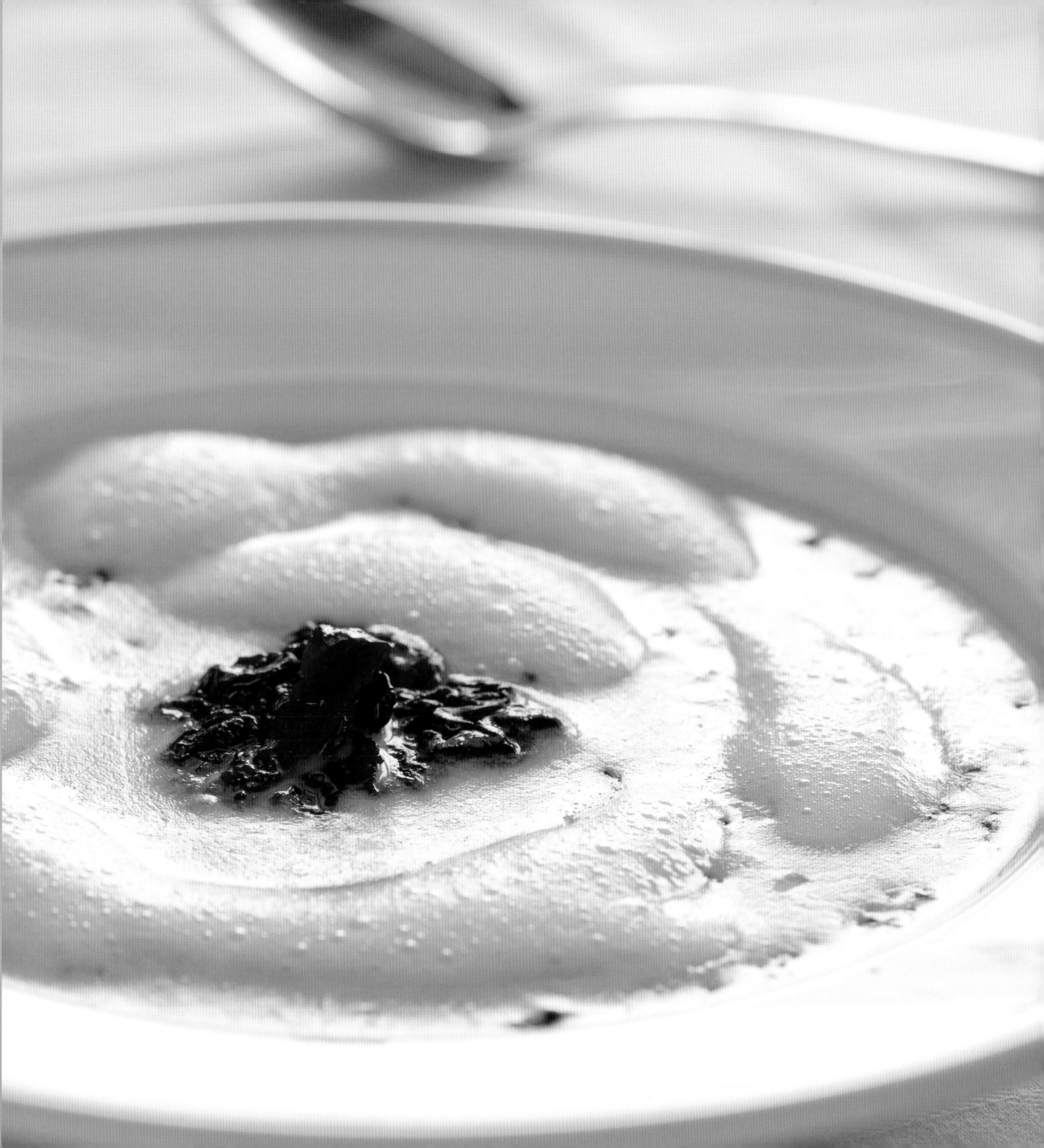

2 cups chopped morel mushrooms

½ cup finely chopped shallots

2 tablespoons extra-virgin olive oil

3 cups chicken or vegetable stock
  (see recipe p. 184)

3 cups heavy cream

4 tablespoons (½ stick) unsalted butter

½ cup crème fraîche

Salt and white pepper

Creamy Morel Soup

Serves 4 to 6

When morels and other forest mushrooms are in season near you, you need to make the most of it. Though dried morels can work too, I like the idea of enjoying this soup as a celebration of the season.

Sauté mushrooms and shallots gently in olive oil in a large saucepot over medium-high heat. Add the stock and simmer until liquid is reduced by half. Add the cream and bring to a gentle boil while stirring, about 10 minutes. Stir in the butter and crème fraîche. Season with salt and white pepper to taste.

2 pounds small calamari

3 cups extra virgin olive oil

1 cup chopped shallots

3 bay leaves

1 tablespoon chopped garlic

1 teaspoon white pepper

1 teaspoon black pepper

2 teaspoons salt

2 tablespoons chopped fresh thyme

2 tablespoons chopped fresh Italian parsley

About ½ pound grape tomatoes

Calamari al Forno

Serves 4 to 6

People are always saying how simple authentic Italian cooking is. If you doubt that for one minute, or if you think simple can't possibly equal good, then give these oven-roasted calamari a try. You might regret all those deep-fried calamari you've put away!

Preheat the oven to 200° F.

Mix all ingredients and spread on a sheet pan. Bake for three hours. Remove from the oven. Drain the olive oil from the top, letting the juice from the calamari remain. Serve hot, lukewarm or cold.

½ cup fennel seeds

1½ pound salmon fillet

¼ cup rock salt

2 tablespoons sugar

Spring mix

DIJON MAYONNAISE:

1 cup mayonnaise

1 tablespoon Dijon mustard

⅓ teaspoon salt

⅓ teaspoon sugar

OVEN-DRIED TOMATOES:

2 tablespoons extra-virgin olive oil

1 clove garlic

2 teaspoons salt

2 tablespoons sugar

½ pound grape tomatoes

1 tablespoon chopped fresh thyme

Black pepper

Salmon Pastrami with Toasted Fennel and Oven-Dried Tomatoes

Serves 4 to 6

More and more restaurants are doing their own curing of fish and meats these days—even calling cured meats by their proper Italian name, *salumi*. This recipe takes an ancient meat technique from Transylvania, making pastrami, and turns its good graces on salmon.

Preheat a dry pan over medium-low heat and toast the fennel seeds. Blend into a powder in a food processor.

Cut salmon fillet in half lengthwise and place on a sheet pan. Coat both sides of the fish with salt and sugar; let cure for 6 hours in the refrigerator.

Sear the fillets about 10 seconds per side on a hot, dry sauté pan. Let cool. Season the fish with fennel powder and wrap it in plastic wrap. Let it rest in the refrigerator for at least 4 hours. Remove plastic wrap and slice into paper-thin strips.

Preheat the oven to 200° F.

Mix all Dijon mayonnaise ingredients in a large bowl.

Spread the olive oil on a sheet pan, and rub the garlic on the sheet pan. Toss 1 teaspoon of the salt and 1 tablespoon of the sugar on top of the oil. Cut the tomatoes in half and place them on the sheet pan. Add the remaining salt and sugar, the thyme and pepper to taste on top of the tomatoes and roast them for 2 hours. Let cool.

Make a mound of spring mix on each plate and top with oven-dried tomatoes. Spoon or squirt (from a plastic bottle) the mayonnaise around the salad. Top with slices of salmon pastrami.

PUMPKIN SAUCE:

1   pound pumpkin or butternut squash, chopped

½   cup chopped shallots

3   cups chicken stock *(see recipe p.184)*

1   cup heavy cream

½   teaspoon ground nutmeg

2   teaspoons of Amaretto liqueur

Salt and black pepper

5   ounces sliced prosciutto or culatello,
    cut in thick strips

1   pound fresh pasta, any shape

½   cup grated Parmesan cheese

Pasta di Zibello

Serves 4

Sometimes I think people don't realize how seasonal the best Italian home cooking tends to be. For every season in the garden, there is a pasta that celebrates what's local and fresh. I think you'll love the taste and the textures of this autumnal dish.

In a large saucepan over medium-high heat, cook the pumpkin, shallots and chicken stock for 30 minutes. Put mixture in a food processor or blender, and mix until smooth. Pour the puree back into the saucepan, and add the cream, nutmeg and Amaretto. Bring to a boil, and season with salt and pepper to taste.

Fry the prosciutto in a dry sauté pan over medium-high heat until crispy.

Cook pasta according to instructions. Drain and toss with pumpkin sauce. Top with Parmesan and crispy prosciutto.

BEURRE BLANC:

1 shallot, finely chopped

4 white peppercorns

1 bay leaf

1 teaspoon fresh thyme

1½ teaspoons white wine vinegar

⅓ cup white wine

⅓ cup heavy cream

2 tablespoons unsalted butter

Salt and white pepper

FISH:

1 cup chopped Italian parsley

Zest of 1 lemon

Juice of 1 lemon

½ teaspoon salt

2 sticks unsalted butter, softened

1 cup fresh green beans

12 small calamari

1½ pounds pike fillets

2 tablespoons extra-virgin olive oil

Pike-Perch with Calamari and Lemon-Parsley Butter

Serves 4

As with many of the fish we love in Finland, there can be a bit of confusion when we translate the names into English. What I call a pike-perch is actually neither a pike nor a perch. It belongs to the Latin genus known as "sander" and most closely resembles an American walleye.

Prepare the beurre blanc. Put the shallots, peppercorns, bay leaf and thyme in a saucepan over high heat. Immediately add the vinegar. Cook for 2 minutes before adding the white wine. Reduce liquid by half. Add the cream and reduce over high heat for about 10 minutes. Strain the sauce into a bowl, then pour it back into the pan. Whisk in the butter. Season with salt and white pepper to taste.

Put chopped parsley, lemon zest, lemon juice and salt into a food processor and mix for 1 to 2 minutes. Add butter and mix until smooth.

Blanch green beans by cooking 3 to 4 minutes in boiling water and immediately plunging into ice water to stop the cooking. Drain the beans.

Cook the calamari and beans in calamari juice.

Sear the fish for 2 minutes, skin side down, in olive oil over medium-high heat. After you carefully turn the fish, sear for 2 minutes on the other side, and drop the butter and parsley atop the crispy skin.

To serve, arrange calamari and beans on a plate. Place fillets on top and spoon on 2 to 3 tablespoons of the beurre blanc.

RISOTTO:

1 pound baby spinach

2 sticks unsalted butter, melted

2 tablespoons extra-virgin olive oil

½ cup finely chopped shallots

2 cups carnaroli or Arborio rice

½ cup white wine

1 quart chicken stock *(see recipe p. 184)*

Salt

½ cup mascarpone cheese

Black pepper

FISH:

1½ pounds whitefish fillets

1 stick unsalted butter, softened

Salt and white pepper

½ cup bread crumbs

GRAPE TOMATOES:

½ pound grape tomatoes, cut in half

½ cup extra-virgin olive oil

Salt and pepper

Coregone Arrosto with Spinach Risotto

Serves 4 to 6

Here's a classic combination from northern Italy. I picture beautiful lakes that reflect the mountains, with storybook villages along the shore. This dish tastes great even without all that, however.

Cook spinach in boiling water for 2 minutes. Squeeze out water. Put hot spinach and melted butter in a blender and blend until smooth.

Heat olive oil and shallots in a saucepan over medium-high heat. After 2 minutes, stir in rice and wine. Add chicken stock and salt to taste. Let the risotto simmer over medium heat for 15 minutes, stirring occasionally. When the liquid has been almost completely absorbed, add mascarpone, black pepper to taste and the spinach puree.

Spread some soft butter on the skin side of fish fillets, and salt and pepper both sides. Place the fillets on a baking sheet. Broil the fillets until golden brown, about 10 minutes. Sprinkle bread crumbs on the skin.

To prepare the grape tomatoes, combine them with the olive oil in a small saucepan over low heat. Simmer for about 10 minutes. Season to taste with salt and pepper.

To serve, spoon the risotto and the tomatoes side by side and top with the fish.

½ cup finely chopped shallots

2 tablespoons extra-virgin olive oil

2 cups carnaroli or Arborio rice

5-6 sprigs saffron

½ cup white wine

1 quart chicken stock

1 stick unsalted butter

½ cup grated Parmesan cheese

Salt and black pepper

SEAFOOD:

12 small calamari

6-8 scallops

1½ teaspoons extra-virgin olive oil

½ tablespoon unsalted butter

Salt and white pepper

CRAWFISH REDUCTION:

1 cup crawfish stock (see recipe p. 185)

1 tablespoon pastis

Salt and white pepper

1 stick unsalted butter

½ cup fresh small shrimp

Risotto di Mare

Serves 4 to 6

The only thing better than creamy, flavorful Italian risotto is creamy, flavorful Italian risotto with fresh local seafood. You can certainly let the seafood in this dish change with your locale and of course with the season.

To prepare the risotto, cook shallots until transparent in olive oil in a saucepan over medium-high heat. Add the rice and saffron after 2 minutes, stirring well. Stir in the wine. Add chicken stock and salt to taste. Let the risotto simmer over medium heat for 15 minutes, stirring occasionally. When the liquid has almost been absorbed, add butter, parmesan and salt and pepper to taste.

Sear the calamari and scallops in a sauté pan with olive oil and butter, about 1 minute per side. Season with salt and white pepper to taste.

Reduce crawfish stock by about half. Season with pastis, salt and pepper. Whisk the butter into the reduction. Add the shrimp and cook for 2 minutes before serving.

Form mounds of risotto on dinner plates. Top with scallops and calamari. Drizzle with the sauce.

1¼ pound burbot or other mild
    freshwater fish fillet

1   tablespoon salt

3   egg whites

1½ cups heavy cream

4   tablespoons bread crumbs

1   tablespoon unsalted butter

MASHED POTATOES:

2   pounds potatoes, peeled

1   cup heavy cream

2   sticks unsalted butter

1-2 teaspoons salt

½   teaspoon white pepper

½   cup finely chopped chives

CARROTS AND ENGLISH PEAS:

1   tablespoon water

4   tablespoons (½ stick) unsalted butter

½   cup diced precooked carrots

½   cup English peas (fresh or frozen)

Salt and white pepper

Burbot Wallenberg with Mashed Potatoes and English Peas

Serves 4

Here's a classic fish mousse combination we love to make at Bucco. With a food processor, it isn't even difficult to make.

Preheat the oven to 300° F.

Dice about 3 ounces of the fillet. Put the rest of the fish in a food processor with salt, and mix for 1 minute, until smooth. Add egg whites one at a time while you continue mixing. Pour in cream, slowly mixing all the time. You should end up with a beautiful fish mousse. Pass the mousse through a food mill or sieve. Mix mousse with diced fillets and divide evenly into four buttered tin molds. Sprinkle bread crumbs on top. Carefully turn upside down in a sauté pan with butter to brown. Put in the oven and bake until temperature reaches 115° F, 15 to 20 minutes.

Cook the potatoes in lightly salted boiling water, until tender. Measure cream and butter into a separate pan and bring to a boil. Add salt and pepper. Press the potatoes one by one into cream-butter mixture, mixing all the time, until you get a fluffy puree. Add the chives just before serving.

To prepare the peas and carrots, bring the tablespoon of water to a boil and instantly whisk the butter in to make a beurre monte emulsion. Add the carrots and peas, cooking for 2 to 3 minutes until heated through. Salt and pepper to taste.

Unmold the fish mousse. Serve the potatoes and the carrot-pea mixture on dinner plates and carefully arrange the mousse on top.

energycuisine

POTATO SALAD:

2   pounds new potatoes, cooked and cooled

1   tablespoon grainy Dijon mustard

½   cup finely chopped shallots

½   cup finely chopped chives

½   cup finely chopped Italian parsley

1   tablespoon finely chopped thyme

1   cup extra-virgin olive oil

½   cup white balsamic vinegar

Salt and black pepper

FISH EGG–SOUR CREAM DRESSING:

1   cup fish eggs

1   cup sour cream

2   tablespoons finely chopped shallots

½   cup finely chopped fresh dill

1   teaspoon salt

½   teaspoon white pepper

SALMON:

1¾ pound salmon fillet, skin on

1   teaspoon salt

½   teaspoon white pepper

Smoked Salmon–New Potato Salad in Fish Egg–Sour Cream Sauce

Serves 4 to 6

Perhaps the most interesting aspect of this satisfying entrée salad is the dressing made with sour cream and fish eggs. The result is subtle, the perfect accompaniment to the smoked salmon.

Slice the potatoes. Mix all salad ingredients in a large bowl. Let rest in the refrigerator for an hour, to balance flavors.

Mix all dressing ingredients in a separate large bowl, and let rest in the refrigerator for an hour.

Sear the salmon skin-side down in a pan. Season with salt and pepper. Set the fish in a cold smoker (including the type that works in the oven); as soon as you notice the first smoke, smoke the salmon 6 to 8 minutes.

Serve pieces of salmon atop the potato salad, drizzled with the dressing.

1¼ pound pike or other mild fish fillet

1   tablespoon salt, plus extra

1   teaspoon freshly ground white pepper,
    plus extra

2   cups heavy cream

HERB CRUST:

1   cup chopped parsley

½   cup chopped dill

1   teaspoon salt

4   slices wheat bread

2   sticks unsalted butter, plus extra

Pike with Pepper and Herb Crust

Serves 4 to 6

This is the fish mousse I trained for six months to make in the Finnish national chefs competition in 2001. I took second place in the semi-finals and then third in the finals. Not so bad for a boy from Pori.

Preheat the oven to 200° F.

Cut a thin section from the edge of the pike fillet (a bone-free area). Cut this part into very thin slices, and season with salt and pepper to taste. Let the slices rest for 15 minutes while you prepare a mousse from the rest of the fillet. Cut the fillet in a few pieces and put them in a food processor with salt and white pepper. While mixing, slowly pour in the cream until a shiny, smooth mousse is formed.

To prepare the herb crust, mix the herbs and salt in a food processor until smooth. Add the bread and mix. Add the 2 sticks of butter and mix until smooth and green. Transfer mixture from food processor to a loaf pan and cover with plastic wrap. Place loaf pan in the refrigerator to get cold, at least 30 minutes.

Butter a different loaf pan by rubbing with room-temperature butter. Alternate layers of the pike slices with layers of the mousse. Cover with aluminum foil and bake until temperature reaches 115° F, about 30 minutes. Remove mousse from pan and set it on a baking sheet. Position a slice of herb crust on top of mousse and broil it until golden brown. Cut into portions and serve.

DUCK:

2 duck breasts

½ teaspoon salt, plus extra

¼ teaspoon white pepper, plus extra

½ teaspoon orange zest

Juice of 1 orange

½ cup honey

4 slices foie gras

SALSIFY:

2 sticks black (or purple) salsify

1 cup heavy cream

½ cup finely chopped shallots

Salt and pepper

½ cup finely chopped fresh chervil

Orange-Glazed Duck Breast with Foie Gras and Black Salsify

Serves 4

Black salsify is also known as Spanish salsify, reflecting its cultural roots in southern Europe. If you can't find black, go with the purple salsify that's more common in North America. It works the same in most recipes.

Preheat the oven to 250° F.

Make shallow cuts along the skin side of the duck breasts to etch in a cross-hatch pattern. Sear the breasts in a sauté pan over high heat until fat melts and skin is golden brown and crispy. Season on both sides with salt and white pepper. Combine the zest and juice of the orange with honey. Glaze the duck skin with the honey-orange mixture. Roast breasts in the oven until internal temperature reaches 130° F, 20 to 25 minutes. Remove duck and let rest for 7 minutes under a piece of aluminum foil. Slice paper-thin across the grain of the meat.

Sear foie gras slices on a hot sauté pan, only 30 seconds on each side. Season with salt and white pepper to taste.

Peel salsify sticks and cook them in boiling water for 5 minutes, until crisp-tender. Cool down immediately in a bowl of ice water. Cut into 3-inch long pieces. Reduce cream with the shallots over medium-high heat. When liquid is reduced by about one third, add salsify. Season with salt and white pepper to taste. Reduce by another third and finish with chervil.

Serve duck breast slices atop the salsify and sauce, with a slice of foie gras on top.

ROASTED VEGETABLES:

1 cup diced carrots

1 cup diced celery root

1 cup diced parsnip

1 cup diced potatoes

1 cup diced shallots

4 tablespoons (½ stick) unsalted butter

½ cup honey

1 teaspoon salt

½ teaspoon black pepper

CHICKEN:

4 chicken breasts

Salt and white pepper

1 cup chopped fresh tarragon

1 tablespoon dried tarragon

1 teaspoon salt

2 sticks unsalted butter, softened

CREAMY COGNAC SAUCE:

1 cup veal demi-glace *(see recipe p. 186)*

½ cup Marsala wine

1 cup heavy cream

¼ cup cognac

1 cup button mushrooms, sautéed

Salt and pepper

Poulet Roti with Creamy Cognac Sauce

Serves 4

I learned this recipe from a dear friend of mine, surgeon Dr. Arno Talvisara, who is passionate about old French recipes. It took me a while to mold this classic into a form that works in our commercial kitchen since we don't have an open wood fire in there! Also, it takes too long to make the dish out of whole chickens, so we use only the breasts.

Preheat the oven to 350° F.

To prepare the roasted vegetables, sauté all the vegetables with butter until tender. Transfer them to a sheet pan. Season with honey, salt and pepper. Bake for 30 minutes, until golden brown.

Sear chicken breasts in a sauté pan over high heat. Season with salt and white pepper.

Combine tarragon and 1 teaspoon salt in a food processor. Add softened butter to processor, and mix until you get a green butter. Glaze the chicken breasts on both sides with tarragon butter. Bake until internal temperature reaches 150° F, about 15 minutes. Let rest for 7 minutes before slicing.

Cook demi-glace and Marsala wine over high heat until liquid is reduced by half. Add the cream and reduce by half again. Add the cognac, mushrooms and salt and pepper to taste, and cook for 10 minutes.

Slice each chicken breast into 2 pieces and position around the vegetables mounded atop a pool of sauce.

½ cup chopped shallots

½ cup chopped fresh thyme

1 tablespoon minced garlic

¼ cup chopped parsley

3 sprigs fresh rosemary

1 cup vegetable oil

2 racks of lamb

⅓ cup veal demi-glace *(see recipe p. 186)*

¼ cup Marsala wine

2 sticks unsalted butter

Salt and pepper

1 cup Japanese (Panko) bread crumbs

Rack of Lamb allo Bucco

Serves 6 to 8

This dish is something that has to be made every time I come to Houston, especially using those beautiful lamb racks I find at Central Market.

Combine shallots, thyme, garlic, parsley, 2 rosemary sprigs and vegetable oil. Rub this mixture over the lamb and let it marinate overnight in the refrigerator.

After marinating, cut the rack into individual chops. Sear on both sides for 3 minutes, over a grill or in a hot pan.

Preheat oven to 300° F.

Heat demi-glace, Marsala wine and the remaining rosemary sprig over medium-high heat until reduced by half. Whisk the butter into the sauce, making a rosemary glaze.

Glaze the chops on both sides. Season with salt and pepper to taste and sprinkle bread crumbs on the top of the fat side. Roast until internal temperature reaches 130° F, about 20 minutes. Take the racks from the oven and let them rest 10 minutes under aluminum foil before serving.

½ cup chopped thyme

½ cup chopped parsley

1 tablespoon dried tarragon

1 tablespoon dried oregano

4 bay leaves

½ cup minced garlic

1 cup chopped shallots

2 tablespoons salt

1 tablespoon black pepper

1 shoulder of lamb

½ cup Marsala wine

2 sprigs rosemary

1 stick unsalted butter

GARLIC MASHED POTATOES:

8 cloves garlic

1 cup milk

2 pounds baking potatoes, peeled

1 cup heavy cream

2 sticks unsalted butter

Salt and white pepper

CARAMELIZED GARLIC:

3 cups water

1 tablespoon salt

1 cup sugar

½ cup white wine vinegar

2 bay leaves

1 teaspoon white peppercorns

3 cups garlic cloves

2 tablespoons unsalted butter

ROSEMARY SAUCE:

1 cup veal demi-glace (see recipe p. 186)

½ cup Marsala wine

2 sprigs rosemary

Rosemary-Glazed Lamb Shoulder with Garlic Mashed Potatoes

Serves 4

Here's a delicious change of pace from lamb racks, chops and legs. Its slow-braised, home-cooked goodness will surely impress your guests.

Preheat the oven to 300° F.

Combine the herbs, garlic, shallots, salt and pepper and rub around the shoulder of lamb. Place in a roasting pan, and cover with water. Braise for 3 hours, then turn shoulder upside down and braise for another 3 hours. Take the shoulder from cooking liquid, debone it and let it cool down so you can cut it into pieces. Strain the lamb juices.

Heat 1 cup of the juices with the Marsala wine over medium-high heat until reduced by one third and turning syrupy. Add rosemary. Whisk in butter while cooking. Glaze the pieces of lamb with rosemary glaze and broil for 2 to 3 minutes. Keep warm.

To make the mashed potatoes, cook garlic cloves in milk for 15 minutes; then blend in a food processor until smooth. Cook the potatoes in lightly salted boiling water. Boil cream and butter in another saucepan. Season with salt and pepper. Mash the potatoes into the cream-butter mixture one at a time until thoroughly incorporated and fluffy. Stir in the pureed garlic before serving.

To make the caramelized garlic, bring the water, salt, sugar, vinegar, bay leaves and white peppercorns to a boil. Strain the liquid into another saucepan, and add garlic cloves. Bring it back to a boil and simmer for 20 to 25 minutes until cloves are well cooked. Transfer garlic cloves and some stock to a small pot, reduce by about half over high heat. Whisk in butter.

Heat all rosemary sauce ingredients over high heat until reduced by half.

Serve the lamb pieces atop the mashed potatoes with caramelized garlic on the side. Spoon the sauce over the top.

1¾ pounds beef tenderloin

Salt and pepper

4 ounces gorgonzola cheese, sliced

POTATOES SABIOSO:

2 pounds new potatoes, peeled

1 tablespoon crushed garlic

½ cup olive oil

1 tablespoon fresh rosemary

½ cup bread crumbs

2 tablespoons salt

1 tablespoon black pepper

Tenderloin of Beef with Gorgonzola and Potatoes Sabioso

Serves 4

The wonderful flavor of Italian gorgonzola cheese is the highlight of this dish for me, giving a special salty tang to this beef tenderloin. The potatoes are a perfect complement.

Preheat the oven to 350° F.

Cut tenderloin in half lengthwise. Then cut the halves into portion-size pieces. Brown the pieces on all sides in a sauté pan, about 3 minutes. Season with salt and pepper. Roast in a skillet or roasting pan until internal temperature of the beef reaches 125° F. Remove from the oven and top each piece with a slice of gorgonzola, and broil until the cheese melts, about 3 to 4 minutes.

Preheat the oven to 375° F.

Cut potatoes into wedges and cook them in boiling water for 5 minutes; drain. Place potato wedges in a baking pan and combine with the rest of the ingredients. Bake until potatoes are golden brown, about 30 minutes.

CULATELLO POTATOES:

4   pounds baking potatoes

2   sticks unsalted butter, melted

1   tablespoon salt

1   teaspoon white pepper

8   paper-thin slices of culatello or prosciutto

½   cup grated Parmesan cheese

½   cup olive oil

STEAK:

2¼ pounds rib-eye steak, 1½ inches thick

1   tablespoon freshly ground black pepper

1   tablespoon freshly ground white pepper

1   tablespoon unsalted butter

1   tablespoon extra-virgin olive oil

1   tablespoon salt

Peppered Rib-Eye with Culatello Potatoes

Serves 4

Standard meat and potatoes have seldom had it so good, thanks to wrapping these potato slices in thin slices of the Italian ham known as culatello. This dish is especially good, I've found, with sautéed mushrooms on the side.

Preheat the oven to 375° F.

Bake potatoes for 50 minutes, until cooked through and springy to the touch. Cut potatoes in half and remove skin. (Wear gloves: the potatoes will be hot!) Place potatoes in a large pot and mash with the melted butter, using a fork. Season with salt and pepper. Spread mashed potatoes in a roasting pan lined with parchment paper. Bake for 15 more minutes, until potato cake is golden brown. Remove from oven and let cool. Carefully turn the pan upside down on a cutting board. Cut the potato cake into portion-size pieces with a sharp knife. Wrap pieces in culatello slices and sprinkle Parmesan and olive oil on top. Bake for another 10 minutes.

Rub the rib-eye steaks with pepper on one side. Sear peppery side in a sauté pan with butter and olive oil over medium-high heat, about 1 minute. Then flip and sear the other side 1 minute more. Put rib-eyes on a sheet pan pepper-side up and season with salt. Roast until internal temperature of the meat reaches 120° F (medium rare), 7 to 8 minutes. Remove steaks from the oven and let them rest for 5 to 7 minutes before serving.

RASPBERRY SORBET:

½ cup sugar

½ cup water

1 cup raspberries

2 tablespoons lemon juice

ORANGE GRANITÉ:

2 cups orange juice

¼ cup sugar

DARK CHOCOLATE MOUSSE:

1 teaspoon powdered gelatin

3 eggs

14 ounces dark chocolate

3 cups heavy cream

WHITE CHOCOLATE MOUSSE:

1 teaspoon powdered gelatin

3 eggs

14 ounces white chocolate

3 cups heavy cream

fresh berries

whipped cream

La Bomba

Serves 4 to 6

The idea for this dessert came from our children. Usually on Sundays, when Bucco is closed, I take the kids to the restaurant with me. In the kitchen, they just love to combine and create new kinds of desserts—chocolates, berries, fruits, ice cream, sorbets. It is so much fun to see these little "chefs" in action, even though they're making a complete mess. With La Bomba, it is all about having fun. I mean, don't you remember Pop Rocks?

RASPBERRY SORBET:

Make a simple syrup by bringing sugar and water to a boil, then let cool. Put all the ingredients in a blender, blending until smooth. Strain raspberry sauce through a sieve to remove seeds. Put in an ice cream machine, following product instructions to make a sorbet. Keep frozen.

ORANGE GRANITÉ:

In a small saucepan, bring orange juice and sugar to boil. Cool down and put in freezer overnight.

DARK CHOCOLATE MOUSSE:

Soak gelatin in cold water for about 5 minutes. Meanwhile, break the eggs into a double boiler and whisk over boiling water until you get a firm foam, not scrambled eggs. Lower the heat. Melt chocolate in another bowl over simmering water. When egg foam is ready, add dissolved gelatin and stir well. Then pour the egg mixture into the chocolate while stirring briskly. Let cool for a few minutes. Whisk cream into loose foam and gently fold into the chocolate mixture. Refrigerate to cool, at least 30 minutes.

WHITE CHOCOLATE MOUSSE:

Soak gelatin in cold water for about 5 minutes. Meanwhile, break the eggs into a double boiler and whisk over boiling water until you get a firm foam, not scrambled eggs. Lower the heat. Melt chocolate in another bowl over simmering water. When egg foam is ready, add dissolved gelatin and stir well. Then pour the egg mixture into the chocolate while stirring briskly. Let cool for a few minutes. Whisk cream into loose foam and gently fold into the chocolate mixture. Refrigerate to cool, at least 30 minutes.

In a dessert glass, build up layers as follows: fresh berries, 1 scoop raspberry sorbet, 1 scoop dark chocolate mousse, 1 scoop orange granité and 1 scoop white chocolate mousse. Sprinkle some Pop Rocks on the white chocolate mousse and cover with whipped cream to hide the pop-rocking surprise.

CHOCOLATE FONDANT:

4 eggs

½ cup sugar

12 tablespoons (1½ sticks) unsalted butter

8 ounces dark chocolate

½ cup potato starch or cornstarch

½ teaspoon baking powder

ORANGE ICE CREAM:

1 cup orange juice

Zest of 1 orange

2½ cups sugar

1 quart heavy cream

1 vanilla bean, cut in half lengthwise

11 egg yolks

CARAMELIZED KUMQUATS:

1 pound kumquats (about 12 kumquats), sliced

1 cup orange juice

1 cup jam sugar with pectin

4 pieces star anise

Chocolate Fondant with Caramelized Kumquats and Orange Ice Cream

Serves 4 to 6

Chocolate and orange, served hot or cold, always make for a sure thing at dessert time. The caramelized kumquats are more than a little bit special.

Preheat the oven to 375° F.

Lightly stir eggs and sugar together in a medium bowl. In a large saucepan, melt butter and chocolate over low heat. Add eggs and sugar, stirring well. Mix starch and baking powder together in a bowl, then add them to the chocolate mixture, stirring briskly. Pour or spoon chocolate fondant base into buttered muffin tins, filling only two thirds of the way. Bake for 10 minutes, until lightly set. When cool, turn the tins upside down on dessert plates.

Start the ice cream by making orange flavor: bring orange juice, zest and 1½ cups of the sugar to a boil. Let cool. In another saucepan, bring the cream, with vanilla bean, to a boil. Meanwhile, in a small bowl, whisk the egg yolks and the remaining 1 cup sugar into a fluffy foam. Pour the boiling cream into the foam and stir briskly. Put egg mixture back in the saucepan and heat to 180° F, stirring constantly. Cool the ice cream base and add the orange flavor. Place mixture in ice cream machine to make an ice cream.

Cook all kumquat ingredients over medium heat for 20 to 30 minutes, until kumquats are coated with syrup. Let cool and spoon around the chocolate fondant, topping with orange ice cream.

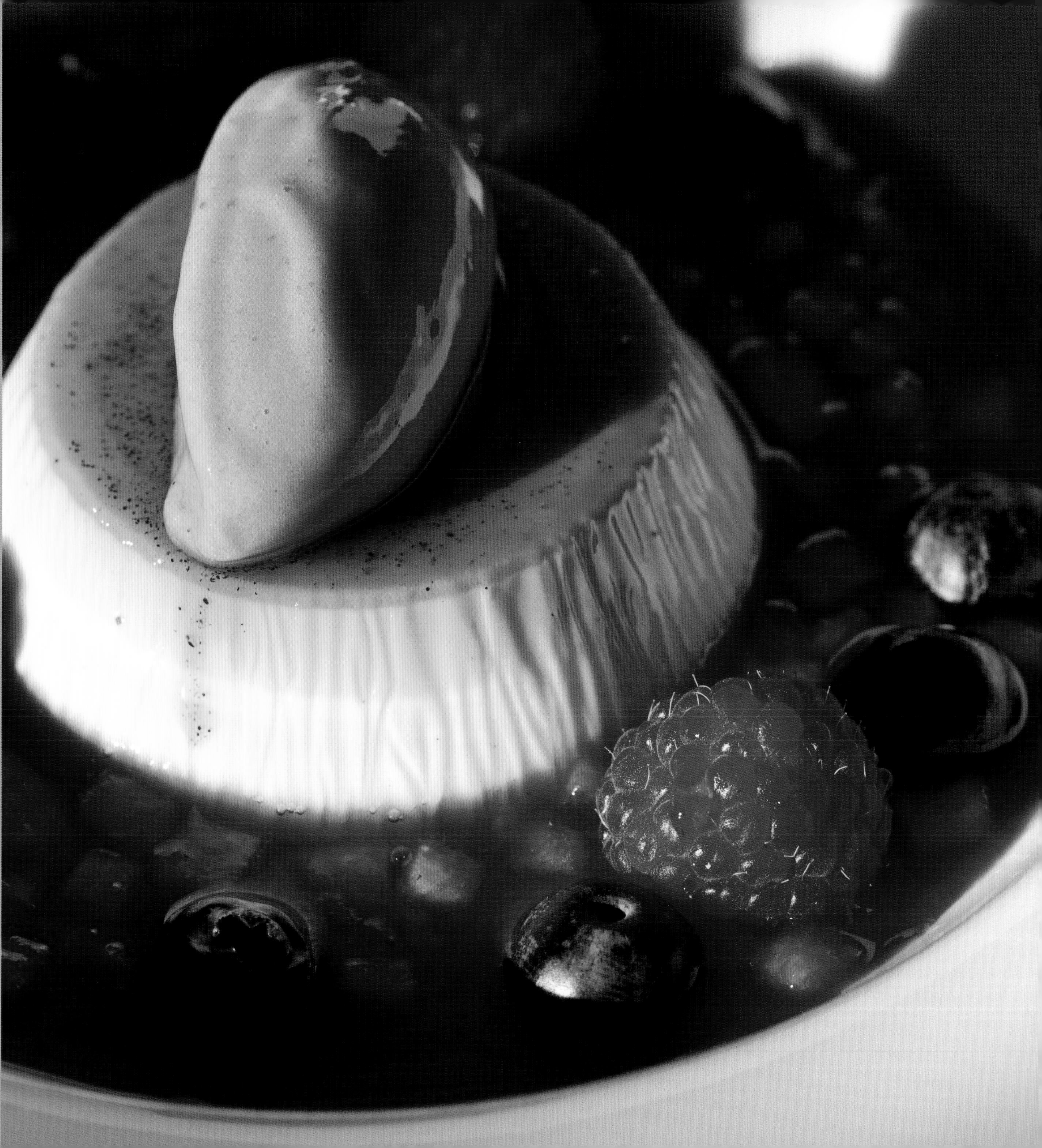

¾ cup sugar

¼ cup water

PANNA COTTA:

3½ cups heavy cream

1 cup whole milk

¾ cup sugar

1 vanilla bean, cut in half lengthwise

¼ cup powdered gelatin

STRAWBERRY JUICE:

2 pounds fresh strawberries

1 cup sugar

½ cup water

Vanilla Panna Cotta with Fresh Strawberries

Serves 12

I made this recipe for the first time during my first trip to Houston. A good friend of mine, Chef Hans Välimäki—who runs his two-Michelin star restaurant, Chez Dominique, in Helsinki, Finland—taught me how to make a perfect panna cotta. The first version was with almonds and rum; this one is spiced with vanilla. Thanks, Hans!

Prepare the sugar glaze by melting and caramelizing sugar in a small saucepan. Heat water and sugar for 5 minutes over medium-high heat, until you get a golden brown syrup. Don't get scared if sugar forms as one piece before it melts into a syrup. Pour the syrup to coat the bottoms of individual muffin tins. Let cool.

Pour cream, milk, sugar and vanilla bean into a medium saucepan, and bring to a boil. Dissolve gelatin in cold water for 5 minutes, then whisk it into the hot panna cotta base. Let the base cool for 20 minutes before you pour it into the muffin tins atop the syrup. Refrigerate for at least 6 hours.

Put all the strawberry juice ingredients in the bowl of a double boiler over boiling water. Juice and color will come out of strawberries. After 30 minutes, strain the juice. Let cool.

To plate the dessert, put tin form upside down and use a knife to free the panna cotta, letting it drop gently on the plate. Serve with berries and juice.

Ingredients

GORGONZOLA ICE CREAM:

1 quart heavy cream
½ teaspoon pure vanilla extract
11 egg yolks
1 cup sugar
10 ounces gorgonzola cheese, grated

GOAT CHEESE ICE CREAM:

1 quart heavy cream
½ teaspoon pure vanilla extract
1 sprig rosemary
11 egg yolks
1 cup sugar
12 ounces fresh goat cheese

PARMIGIANO ICE CREAM:

1 quart heavy cream
½ teaspoon pure vanilla extract
11 egg yolks
1 cup sugar
12 ounces parmigiano, grated

CARAMELIZED BEETS:

2 cups sugar
1 cup Port wine
2 cups peeled and finely diced beets, about 2 beets
1 cinnamon stick
4 pieces star anise

CARAMELIZED FIGS:

2 cups sugar
1 cup Marsala wine
1 vanilla bean, cut in half lengthwise
2 cups sliced figs

RED TOMATO JAM:

3 cups cherry or grape tomatoes, cut in half
1¼ cups sugar
1 teaspoon salt
Zest of half a lemon
1 teaspoon green peppercorns
1 sprig rosemary

Three Cheese Ice Creams with Three Toppings

Serves 8

Cheese ice creams are something that we usually serve after the main course. Guests often wonder how we make these fabulous ice creams with authentic cheese flavors. As a practical matter, here's a series of six component recipes with guidance on assembling them on one plate at the end.

GORGONZOLA ICE CREAM:

Pour the cream and vanilla into a medium saucepan and bring to a boil. In a bowl, whisk egg yolks and sugar into a fluffy foam. Pour the boiling cream into the bowl and stir briskly. Pour the base back into the saucepan and heat to 180° F, stirring constantly. Add the gorgonzola cheese and let it melt. Let cool and make ice cream with ice cream machine.

GOAT CHEESE ICE CREAM:

Pour the cream, vanilla and rosemary into a medium saucepan and bring to a boil. In a bowl, whisk egg yolks and sugar into a fluffy foam. Pour the boiling cream into the bowl and stir briskly. Pour the base back into the saucepan and heat to 180° F, stirring constantly. Add the goat cheese and let it melt. Let cool and make ice cream with ice cream machine.

PARMIGIANO ICE CREAM:

Pour the cream and vanilla into a medium saucepan and bring to a boil. In a bowl, whisk egg yolks and sugar into a fluffy foam. Pour the boiling cream into the bowl and stir briskly. Pour the base back into the saucepan and heat to 180° F, stirring constantly. Add the parmigiano and let it melt. Let cool and make ice cream with ice cream machine.

CARAMELIZED BEETS:

Melt and caramelize sugar in a saucepan over medium heat, until golden brown and bubbly. Stir in the wine and cook for 2 to 3 minutes. Add the rest of the ingredients and cook for 30 minutes over low heat, until beets are caramelized and tender. Let cool.

CARAMELIZED FIGS:

Melt and caramelize sugar in a saucepan over medium heat, until golden brown and bubbly. Stir in the wine and vanilla bean, and cook for 2 to 3 minutes. Add the figs and cook over low heat for 15 to 20 minutes, until figs are caramelized and tender. Let cool.

RED TOMATO JAM:

Put all ingredients in a medium saucepan, bring to a boil and let simmer for 30 to 40 minutes. Let cool.

To assemble the dessert on a large plate or bowl, serve the gorgonzola ice cream atop the beets, the goat cheese ice cream atop the figs and the parmigiano ice cream atop the tomato jam.

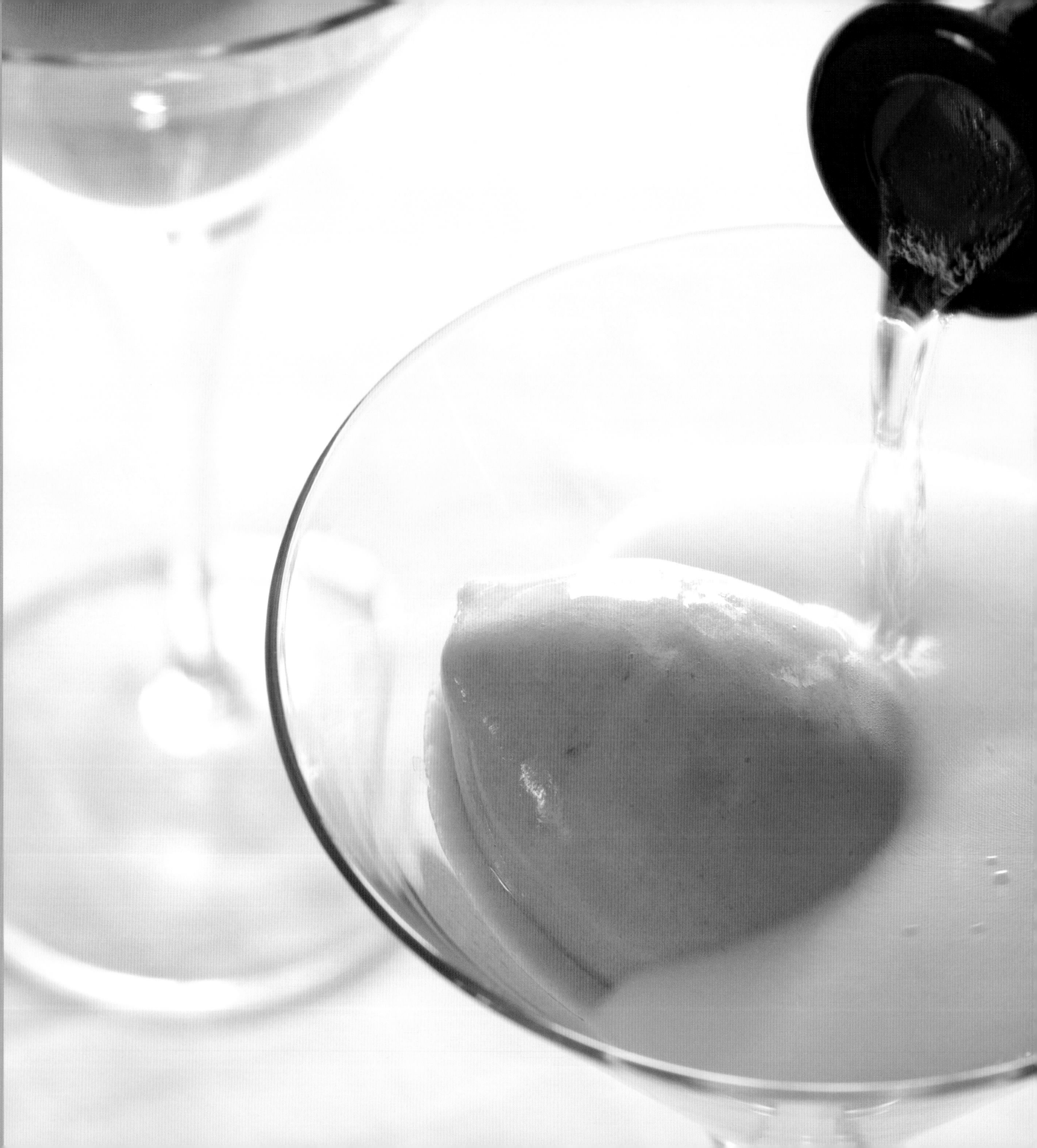

1 cup sugar

1 cup water

2 cups pureed white peaches

2 tablespoons lime juice

Champagne or sparkling wine

Sorbetto Bellini

Serves 4 to 6

I got this idea for a Bellini sorbet, of course, after visiting Harry's Bar in Venice, where the legendary white peach and Champagne cocktail was invented.

Make a simple syrup by bringing the sugar and water to a boil, then allowing it to cool. Mix syrup, peaches and lime juice together and make a sorbet in ice cream machine.

Scoop one ball of sorbet into a cocktail glass and pour a dash of Champagne on top.

4 ounces white chocolate

10 ounces dark chocolate

1¼ cups crème fraîche

2 tablespoons Calvados brandy

1 cup cocoa powder

Chocolate Truffles

Serves 6

A good recipe for chocolate truffles is a must. Especially under the Christmas tree—and for chocoholics, all year round. This is the easiest recipe there is.

Put chocolates and crème fraîche in the bowl of a double boiler over simmering water. Stir occasionally until chocolate melts. Stir in Calvados. Cool down in the refrigerator, at least 2 hours. Then shape the chocolate mixture into tiny truffles by hand. Dust with cocoa powder before serving.

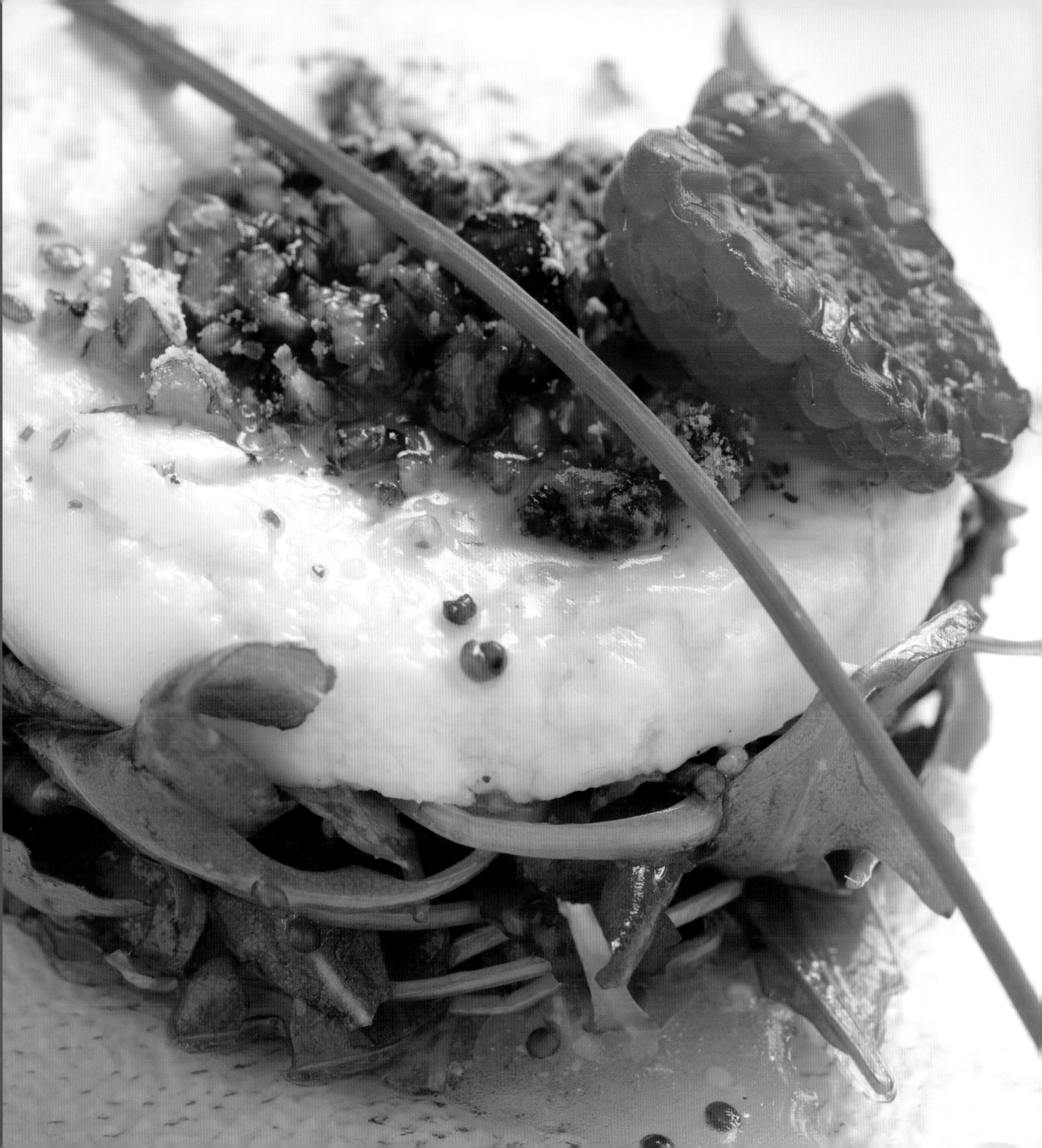

SALAD:

8 (¼-inch) slices Bucheron goat cheese

8 cups arugula

¼ cup chopped pecans, toasted

8 sprigs chives, to garnish

4 fresh raspberries, cut in half, to garnish

VINAIGRETTE:

½ teaspoon whole-grain mustard

2 tablespoons water

1 tablespoon white balsamic vinegar

1½ teaspoons lavender honey

1½ teaspoons chopped shallot

¼ cup Shiner blonde beer

¼ teaspoon kosher salt

White pepper

¼ cup extra-virgin olive oil

Arugula Salad with Warm Goat Cheese and Shiner Honey–Lavender Vinaigrette

Serves 8

As part of the menu we created inspired by our visit to the wonderful Spoetzel Brewery in Shiner, Texas, we came up with the idea of incorporating beer into the dressing for this salad of tangy arugula and warm goat cheese.

Preheat the oven to 375° F.

Bake goat cheese slices for about 4 minutes, until they start to melt.

In a small bowl, place the whole-grain mustard, water, vinegar, honey, shallot, beer, salt and a pinch of white pepper. Whisk together for 1 minute. Then slowly add olive oil, whisking constantly. Check your seasoning.

Put arugula in a bowl and add the vinaigrette (3 to 4 tablespoons per serving). Mix gently with tongs.

Mold the salad in the center of a plate with a dough cutter. Gently place the goat cheese on top of the salad. Sprinkle pecans on top of the goat cheese. Garnish with chives and raspberries.

16 large neck clams

2 tablespoons unsalted butter

½ cup chopped shallot

1 cup diced carrot

1 cup diced celery

1 (12-ounce) bottle Shiner Bock beer

1 cup water

1 cup white wine

½ teaspoon kosher salt

White pepper

2 cups Japanese (Panko) bread crumbs

2 cups rock salt

1 sprig fresh rosemary

10 black peppercorns

10 cloves

½ bunch cilantro

Shiner Clams Gratinée

Serves 4

A bit more beer from our Shiner trip, about a two-hour drive west from Houston, turns up in the crisp, golden-brown topping on this baked clam favorite.

Soak the clams in a pot of cold water. Then brush them one by one and soak them again for 20 minutes in a fresh pot of water. In a large sauté pan, add 1 tablespoon of the butter, plus the shallot, carrot and celery and cook over low heat until light brown, 3 to 5 minutes. Place the clams on top, add the Shiner beer, water and white wine. Cover the sauté pan with a lid. Cook for 10 to 15 minutes, until all the clams are open. Remove clams from the pan.

Reduce the remaining liquid by half. Whisk in ½ tablespoon of the butter. Season with kosher salt and a pinch of white pepper, and set aside.

Meanwhile, melt the last ½ tablespoon of butter and mix it with the bread crumbs in a bowl. Split the clams in half, keeping only the half shells with clams on them. Cover the top of each clam with a teaspoon of bread crumb mixture. Place them on a sheet pan and set under a pre-heated broiler for 5 to 8 minutes, until golden brown.

To serve, mix rock salt, rosemary, peppercorns and cloves in a bowl. Spread this mixture on the bottom of plates and top each with 4 clams (the salt mixture will help keep the clams from sliding). Sprinkle the top of the clams with cilantro. Serve immediately.

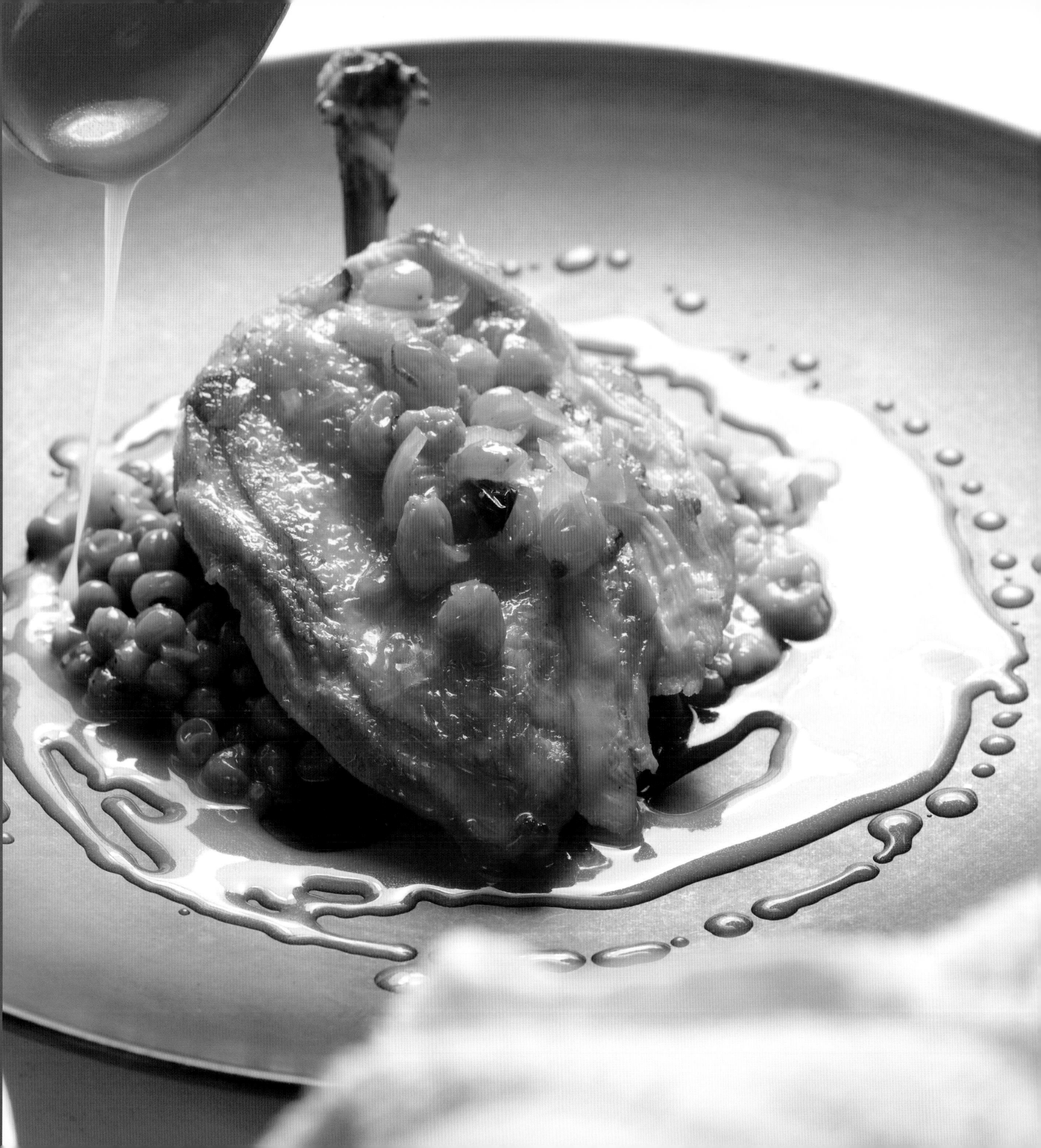

CHICKEN:

4   free-range chicken breasts

2   tablespoons unsalted butter

1   cup chopped shallots

¼   cup golden raisins

2   tablespoons white balsamic vinegar

1   bottle Shiner beer

Salt and white pepper

RISOTTO:

2   tablespoons extra-virgin olive oil

½   cup finely chopped shallots

2   cups carnaroli or Arborio rice

3   cups Shiner dark beer

1   cup chicken stock *(see recipe p. 184)*

Salt and pepper

½   cup heavy cream

½   cup grated parmigiano

FRICASSEE:

1   tablespoon Shiner dark beer

4   tablespoons (½ stick) unsalted butter

1   cup English peas (fresh or frozen)

1   cup finely chopped carrots

Salt and white pepper

Roasted Free-Range Chicken with Shiner Risotto and English Pea Fricassee

Serves 4

Finally from our special Shiner beer menu, it's pretty hard to beat the extra suggestion of flavor the dark beer brings to this risotto. Besides that, everybody loves our roasted chicken.

Preheat the oven to 350° F.

Sear chicken breasts in a sauté pan with butter. Add shallots and raisins, browning for 2 to 3 minutes. Add the vinegar and beer, seasoning with salt and white pepper to taste. Transfer the chicken breasts to a sheet pan and pour shallot-raisin mixture over the top. Bake in the oven until the temperature of the chicken reaches 150° F. Let it rest for 7 minutes before serving.

Meanwhile, prepare the risotto by heating olive oil and shallots in a saucepan. Add the rice after 2 minutes, stirring well. Pour in the beer, chicken stock and salt to taste. Let the risotto simmer over medium heat for 15 minutes, stirring occasionally. When the liquid has been almost absorbed, add the cream, parmigiano and black pepper to taste. Cook 2 more minutes to melt cheese and absorb cream.

Make the pea fricassee by bringing the beer to a boil and instantly whisk in the butter to make a beer monte emulsion. Add the peas and carrots, cooking until tender, 3 to 4 minutes. Salt and pepper to taste.

PASTIS BOUILLABAISSE:

1   tablespoon extra-virgin olive oil

1   shallot, minced

1   tablespoon tomato paste

¼   cup pastis

1½ teaspoons minced garlic

2   tablespoons white wine

1   cup crawfish stock *(see recipe p. 185)*

SAFFRON ROUILLE POTATO SAUCE:

2   tablespoons fingerling potatoes, cooked and
    mashed

1   teaspoon minced garlic

1   egg yolk

1   teaspoon saffron powder

½   teaspoon salt

½   teaspoon pepper

1   teaspoon Dijon mustard

1   tablespoon extra-virgin olive oil

3   tablespoons vegetable oil

4   large (U-10) scallops

1   teaspoon sea salt

½   teaspoon white pepper

1   leek, julienned, for garnish

Pan-Seared Scallops with Saffron Rouille Potato and Pastis Bouillabaisse Sauce

Serves 4

Any recipe that incorporates rouille, bouillabaisse and pastis is about as Provençal as you can get. In honor of the seafood stew world-famous as bouillabaisse, we produced here instead an intense seafood sauce that's spooned around seafood. Trust us, it's delicious.

To prepare the pastis bouillabaisse, pour olive oil in a large sauté pan, add the shallot and cook until lightly caramelized. Add tomato paste and flambé with pastis, then add garlic, white wine and crawfish stock. Simmer for 15 minutes over low heat and pass through a fine sieve.

To prepare the saffron sauce, place the mashed cooked fingerling potatoes in a metallic bowl. Add garlic, egg yolk, saffron, salt and pepper. Slowly incorporate the Dijon mustard. Then gently whisk, adding the olive oil first and then the vegetable oil to the mashed potato mixture until the consistency is smooth and thick.

Salt and pepper the scallops with sea salt and white pepper, then pan sear each side for 2 minutes in a sauté pan.

Place the rouille potatoes in the middle of a plate. Place the scallops on top of the potatoes. Surround with pastis bouillabaisse sauce. Top the scallops with leeks to garnish.

DOUGH:

1   egg

1   quart all-purpose flour

Kosher salt

2   cups water

1   tablespoon extra-virgin olive oil

STUFFING:

3   cups ground veal

1   cup ground ham

½   tablespoon unsalted butter

1   onion, finely chopped

2   cups cooked spinach

½   teaspoon kosher salt

½   teaspoon white pepper

4   eggs, beaten

½   cup extra-virgin olive oil

1   tablespoon rock salt

1½ teaspoons vegetable oil

Prepared marinara or other tomato sauce

Aged Parmesan cheese

Meme's Ravioli

Serves 8

Nobody can make ravioli quite like David's Meme (grandmother), home in Provence. That's why we drafted no less an authority than Meme herself to teach us how to make her all-time signature dish.

In the bowl of a stand mixer, prepare the dough by combining the egg, flour, a pinch of salt, water and olive oil. Mix on low speed until a ball shape forms. Let it rest for 1 hour before shaping as ravioli.

Combine ground veal and ground ham. Sauté chopped onion in butter until it begins to caramelize, then briefly sauté the meat. Add spinach and cook just until limp, 2 to 3 minutes. Season with salt and pepper. Cook 2 to 3 minutes more for the flavors to meld. Let cool. Mix in the eggs until thoroughly incorporated. Add olive oil and combine.

Roll out some of the dough to ⅛ inch thick. Spoon a long line of the stuffing across the dough and then fold the dough across the stuffing to cover. Using your fingers, squeeze the dough around the stuffing to form small (1- to 2-inch) dumplings, tearing off each to separate from the line. Save the excess dough and use it for the next batch, rolling out more pasta sheets.

In a large pot, bring water to a boil with the rock salt and vegetable oil. Cook ravioli in batches for about 2 minutes. Remove them gently with a slotted spoon and spread them on a long dish with tomato sauce. Sprinkle with aged Parmesan.

SEA BASS:

½ teaspoon kosher salt

1   pinch white pepper

4   (6-ounce) Chilean sea bass fillets

1   tablespoon unsalted butter

¼ cup Japanese (Panko) bread crumbs

1   tablespoon plus 1 teaspoon salmon eggs, to garnish

BEURRE MONTE:

Juice of 1 lemon

¼ cup water

¼ cup white wine

Salt and pepper

4   tablespoons (½ stick) unsalted butter

1   teaspoon heavy cream

ASPARAGUS FRICASSEE:

½ bunch asparagus

½ tablespoon unsalted butter

1   tablespoon minced shallots

½ teaspoon kosher salt

White pepper

1 tablespoon chopped fresh Italian parsley

Crusted Chilean Sea Bass with Asparagus Fricassee

Serves 4

In professional kitchens, searing fish for a crispy outside and then baking it for a moist inside is one of the oldest tricks in the book. We hope this wonderful, rather simple dish, with its flavorful fricassee of asparagus, will make a believer out of you.

Preheat the oven to 350° F.

Salt and pepper the sea bass. Melt ½ tablespoon of the butter in a sauté pan, and sear each side of the fish for 2 minutes over low heat until a nice crust forms. Let the fish cool. In a bowl, combine the remaining ½ tablespoon of butter and bread crumbs. Place the bread crumb mixture on top of each cooled fish. Transfer the fish to a sheet pan.

To prepare the beurre monte, put everything except butter and heavy cream in a saucepan. Reduce it by three quarters over low heat. Add heavy cream and slowly whisk in the butter. Check salt and pepper.

To make the asparagus fricassee, thinly slice the asparagus on a diagonal. Melt the butter in a sauté pan and sweat shallots until light gold. Add asparagus on top of the shallots, along with salt and a pinch of white pepper. Sauté for 2 to 3 minutes, then sprinkle with Italian parsley. Keep warm.

Bake the fish for 8 minutes.

To serve, carefully set the fish on top of the fricassee, with a teaspoon of salmon eggs for garnish. Spoon warm beurre monte around the top and sides.

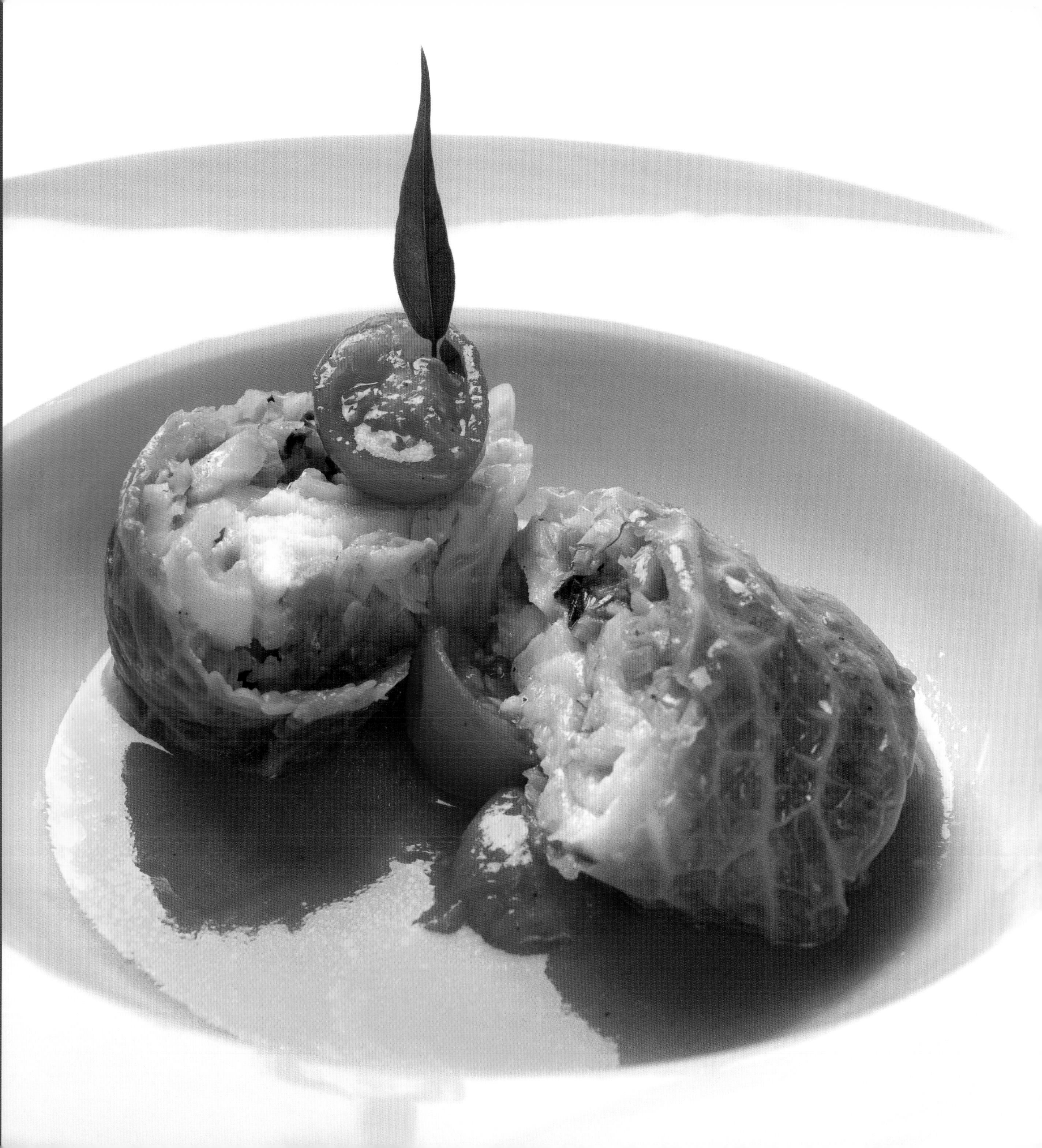

4   big leaves of winter cabbage

½   cup finely chopped winter cabbage

½   cup finely chopped fennel bulb

½   cup finely chopped shallots

½   cup finely chopped carrots

2   tablespoons finely chopped celery

1   tablespoon finely chopped Italian parsley

4   tablespoons (½ stick) unsalted butter

2   tablespoons extra-virgin olive oil

Salt and white pepper

4   small fillets of rascasse, or other white fish

BEURRE MONTE:

2   tablespoons water

1   stick unsalted butter

GRAPE TOMATOES:

1½ cups grape tomatoes

½   cup extra-virgin olive oil

Salt and pepper

Rascasse Fillet Wrapped in Winter Cabbage

Serves 4

This dish came together quickly during one of our cooking-and-photography sessions in deep Provence. Though that would clearly be David's world, it was Jani who took home the applause for a notion that began when he spotted winter cabbage at the open-air market along the waterfront that morning.

Preheat the oven to 300° F.

Blanch the cabbage leaves in boiling water for 5 minutes. Immediately plunge into ice water. Strain the water from the cabbage.

Sauté all the chopped vegetables and herbs with butter and olive oil for 5 to 7 minutes, until softened. Season with salt and white pepper to taste.

Meanwhile, prepare the beurre monte by bringing the water to a boil. Whisk in the butter a little at a time.

Cut grape tomatoes in half, combine them with olive oil, and salt and pepper to taste. Simmer in a saucepan over low heat for 10 minutes.

Start the cabbage roll by placing a tablespoon of vegetables on top of each cabbage leaf. Then salt and pepper the fish, setting it atop the vegetables. Glaze the fish fillet with beurre monte. Wrap it into a roll. Place in a baking pan and bake for 12 to 15 minutes. Serve with grape tomatoes on top and sides.

QUAIL BREAST:

4   double quail breasts

½   teaspoon kosher salt

⅛   teaspoon black pepper

4   tablespoons ground chorizo sausage

4   tablespoons plum preserves

4   slices bacon

FOIE GRAS:

4   (2-ounce) slices foie gras

Salt and pepper

CELERY ROOT PUREE:

3   cups whole milk

3   cups water

1   tablespoon salt, plus extra

2   large celery roots (about 2½ pounds total), peeled and cut into ½-inch cubes

1   medium russet potato, peeled and cut into ½-inch cubes

1   small onion, peeled and quartered

5   tablespoons unsalted butter, cut into 5 pieces

Ground white pepper

Sage leaves, for garnish

Roasted Quail Breast with Plum and Chorizo Filling

Serves 4

The chorizo brings "salty" to the table, while the plum preserves bring "sweet." Together, we've found they make a wonderful stuffing for quail breasts. They also are excellent for keeping the meat from even thinking about drying out during the cooking process.

Preheat the oven to 350° F.

Spread quail breasts out on a clean, dry work surface. Season with salt and pepper on both sides. Spread 1 tablespoon of chorizo on each and spread the plum on top of the chorizo. Close up each breast and wrap tightly with a bacon slice. Bake for 15 minutes.

While the quail is baking, preheat a sauté pan. Salt and pepper the foie gras slices and sear them for 30 seconds on each side.

To make the celery puree, bring milk, water and salt just to a boil in a heavy saucepan over high heat. Add celery root cubes, potato cubes and onion quarters, and bring to a boil. Reduce heat to medium and simmer until vegetables are tender, about 30 minutes. Drain, discarding cooking liquid. Combine vegetables and butter in a food processor and puree until smooth. Season to taste with salt and white pepper.

Serve quail with puree on the side, topped with the foie gras. Garnish with sage.

1   rabbit, cut into 4 pieces

½   cup extra-virgin olive oil, plus extra

½   cup diced onion

½   cup diced carrot

½   cup diced celery

4   cloves garlic, crushed

2   tablespoons all-purpose flour

2   cups Madeira wine

2   cups tomato coulis (*see recipe p. 186*)

2   cups water

1   tablespoon chopped fresh thyme

1½ teaspoons chopped fresh rosemary

½   teaspoon kosher salt, plus extra

¼   teaspoon black pepper, plus extra

1   cinnamon stick

Wood-Oven Rabbit Etouffee

Serves 4

We were lucky enough to cook this terrific braised rabbit in a wood-burning oven in Provence, with all the extra flavors the fire and smoke impart. Obviously, it will be almost as good served piping hot from any kind of oven. This rabbit pairs beautifully with fresh pasta or polenta.

Preheat the oven to 300° F.

Salt and pepper the rabbit. Coat a thick cast iron Dutch oven with olive oil and cook rabbit for 10 to 15 minutes, until golden brown. Remove the rabbit from the Dutch oven. In the same pot, pour more olive oil and sauté onion, carrot, celery and garlic until they begin to caramelize. Return rabbit to the pot, on top of the vegetables, and sprinkle with flour. Cook for 2 minutes, stirring occasionally. Deglaze with Madeira wine until liquid is reduced by half.

Add tomato coulis, water, thyme, rosemary, salt, pepper and cinnamon stick, and cover. Place the pot in the oven and bake for an hour and a half, occasionally checking the thickness of the sauce. Add water if necessary. Remove the pot from the oven and let rest for 20 minutes with the lid on before serving.

1¼ pound king salmon fillet

¼ cup rock salt

2 tablespoons sugar

MOSAIC:

½ cup finely chopped green bell pepper

½ cup finely chopped carrots

½ cup finely chopped shallots

½ cup finely chopped fennel bulb

2 tablespoons lemon juice

2 tablespoons chopped chives

1 cup extra-virgin olive oil

Salt and pepper

2 tablespoons fish eggs, preferably salmon

King Salmon Gravlax with Vegetable Mosaic

Serves 8

There probably aren't a lot of vegetable mosaics served on oil platforms out in the Gulf of Mexico—or a whole lot of gravlax either, for that matter. But that's what we cooked at the invitation of our good friends at Technip. They flew us by helicopter about 130 miles south of Galveston to cook a four-course lunch for the men who work there. You don't really know what small looks like till you're trying to aim at an oil platform (actually quite large) from the sky above the vast blue expanse of the Gulf.

Cure the fillet of fish with salt and sugar overnight. Cut into thin slices.

Prepare mosaic salad by mixing all the chopped vegetables in a bowl. Toss with lemon juice, chives and olive oil. Salt and pepper to taste. Let salad rest for one hour before serving. Add the slices of fish just before serving and garnish with fish eggs.

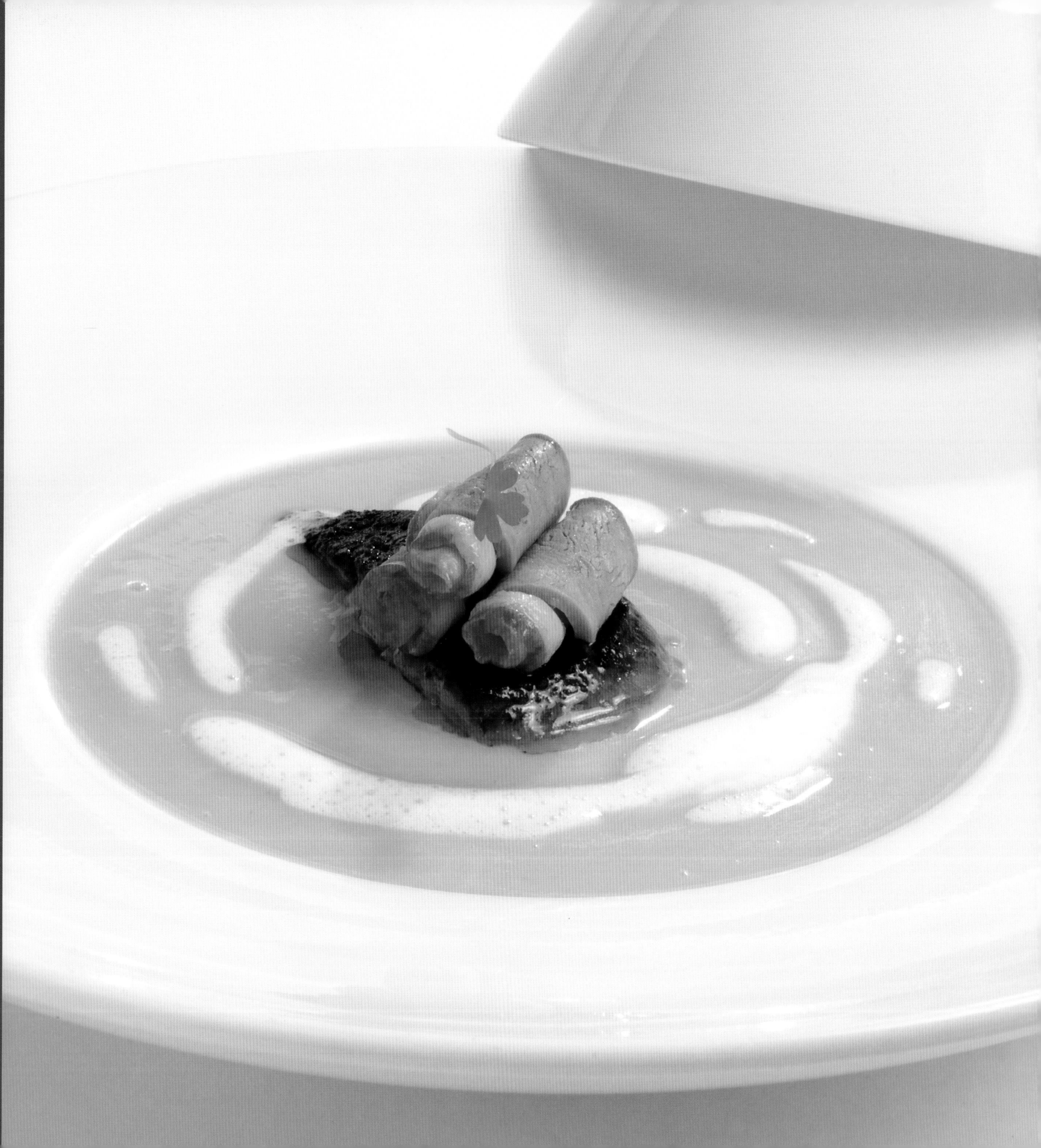

½ pound Jerusalem artichokes

2 shallots, peeled and chopped

1 quart chicken stock *(see recipe p. 184)*

1 quart heavy cream

½ teaspoon kosher salt, plus extra

White pepper

4 (1½-ounce) slices foie gras

6 ounces smoked duck breast

Jerusalem Artichoke Soup with Smoked Duck Breast and Seared Foie Gras

Serves 4

From the menu we cooked out in the Gulf of Mexico, celebrating the oil rig spar produced in Pori by our good friends at Technip—thus also celebrating our personal and professional friendship—here's a soup that's as easy to make as its smoked duck and foie gras upgrades are spectacular.

Peel the artichokes and slice them. Place the artichokes, shallots, chicken stock, heavy cream, salt and a pinch of white pepper in a stock pot. Bring to a boil and reduce heat to simmer for 30 minutes. Blend everything together in a food processor and pass through a fine sieve. Keep soup warm.

Season the foie gras with salt and white pepper to taste. Heat a dry sauté pan over high heat, then add the slices of foie gras and pan sear them for 15 seconds on each side.

Slice the duck breast in thin slices and place them on top of the pan-seared foie gras. Serve with the soup.

1 cup dried morels or other dried mushrooms

½ teaspoon kosher salt, plus extra

Black pepper

1 (6-pound) center-cut beef tenderloin

1 tablespoon unsalted butter

1 pound puff pastry

1 egg yolk, beaten

SAUCE:

1 cup dried morels or other dried mushrooms

1 tablespoon chopped shallots

1 teaspoon unsalted butter

¼ cup cognac

1 cup veal stock *(see recipe p. 186)*

1 cup heavy cream

½ teaspoon kosher salt

White pepper

Smoked Beef Tenderloin Wellington

Serves 4

Just to show our appreciation, this was the main course we served that day on the oil platform far out in the Gulf of Mexico, right after the cured king salmon gravlax and the lush veloute soup of Jerusalem artichokes.

Preheat the oven to 350° F.

Rehydrate the morels or other dried mushrooms in a bowl of water for about 10 minutes, then drain them. Salt and pepper the tenderloin. Pan sear the tenderloin, then let cool. Chop the mushrooms. Melt the butter in a sauté pan and sauté the mushrooms over low heat until all the water cooks out. Season with salt and a pinch of pepper. Let cool.

Lay down the puff pastry, about ½ inch thick. Put the mushroom duxelle on top of the puff pastry, place the tenderloin on top of the duxelle and roll the pastry around it to form a thick log. Brush the pastry with the egg yolk. Bake the Wellington until the inside meat temperature reaches 125° F. Take the Wellington out of the oven and let it rest for 10 minutes before slicing.

Meanwhile, prepare the sauce. Sauté the rehydrated mushrooms and the shallots in butter until golden. Carefully flambé with cognac and cook until dry. Add veal stock, reducing liquid by half. Add cream and reduce by two thirds. Season with salt and a pinch of white pepper.

Serve slices of wellington with morel sauce spooned over the top.

1   (3-pound) deboned leg of wild boar,
    cut in 1½-inch cubes
2   bottles dry red wine
2   carrots, peeled and diced
1   onion, diced
4   stalks celery, chopped
5   cloves garlic, chopped
1   sprig fresh rosemary
1   tablespoon chopped fresh thyme
2   bay leaves
½   cup vegetable oil
3   tablespoons all-purpose flour
2   cups veal stock
1   quart water
2   tablespoons blueberry jelly or jam
2   teaspoons kosher salt, plus extra
⅛   teaspoon pepper, plus extra
Fresh pasta, cooked al dente

Wild Boar Daube Provençal

Serves 6

Though it's an odd-sounding (and odd-looking) word, a daube in French is nothing more than a stew that cooks down until it's practically one tender thing. In some parts of the South of France, daubes are made using bulls from the bullfighting festivals. Using marinated wild boar meat cut into cubes, we stopped far short of having to face any dangerous horns.

Place cubed boar meat in a large bowl with the red wine, carrots, onion, celery, garlic, rosemary, thyme and bay leaves. Cover the bowl with plastic wrap and marinate in the refrigerator for 24 hours.

Strain the marinade from the meat and reserve. Separate all vegetables from the meat in two large bowls. (Squeeze the meat cubes with your hands to remove the extra wine.)

Heat about half the vegetable oil in a large pan over high heat. Brown the meat, seasoning lightly with salt and pepper. Remove the meat from the pan.

In the same pan, sauté all vegetables until lightly caramelized.

Pour the remaining vegetable oil into a large, heavy stock pot and add the browned meat. Sprinkle flour on top of the meat and stir for 10 minutes until the flour starts to brown. Add the vegetables, marinade, veal stock, water, blueberry jam, 2 teaspoons of salt and ⅛ teaspoon pepper. Lower heat and cook slowly until meat is tender.

Remove only the meat from the pot and set aside at room temperature. Raise the heat to medium-high and reduce the liquid with the vegetables until syrupy, about an hour and a half. Pass the contents of the pot through a fine sieve, pressing the vegetables with a wooden spoon. Discard the vegetables left in the sieve. Return the meat back to the sauce and warm for 10 minutes. Serve pieces of daube over fresh pasta.

1   red onion

1   yellow onion

2   green bell peppers

2   red bell peppers

2   yellow bell peppers

2   large zucchini

1   large eggplant

1½ cups extra-virgin olive oil

Kosher salt and black pepper

1   teaspoon chopped fresh rosemary

1   teaspoon chopped fresh thyme

2   cups fresh basil leaves

1   tablespoon crushed garlic

1   cup tomato coulis (*see recipe p. 186*)

1   slice fresh bacon, diced (optional)

Provençal Ratatouille

Serves 8

It's funny: just about every cook in America thinks he or she knows how to make ratatouille, especially after that animated film about the rat who wants to be a chef. Put a bunch of vegetables in a pot of water and cook until done, right? Wrong. There's actually a good deal of science—and some serious timing—involved in how real ratatouille is made in Provence.

Chop all vegetables into 1-inch pieces. Sauté the vegetables one by one in 1 cup of the olive oil, sprinkling with salt and pepper, in the following order: red and yellow onion together; green, red and yellow bell peppers together; zucchini and eggplant. In a thick—preferably cast iron—pot, combine the vegetables with the remaining olive oil and the chopped bacon. Add rosemary and thyme. Cover and simmer over low heat for 1 hour. Add fresh basil, garlic and tomato coulis. Adjust seasoning with salt and pepper. Cook for another 15 minutes to let flavors meld.

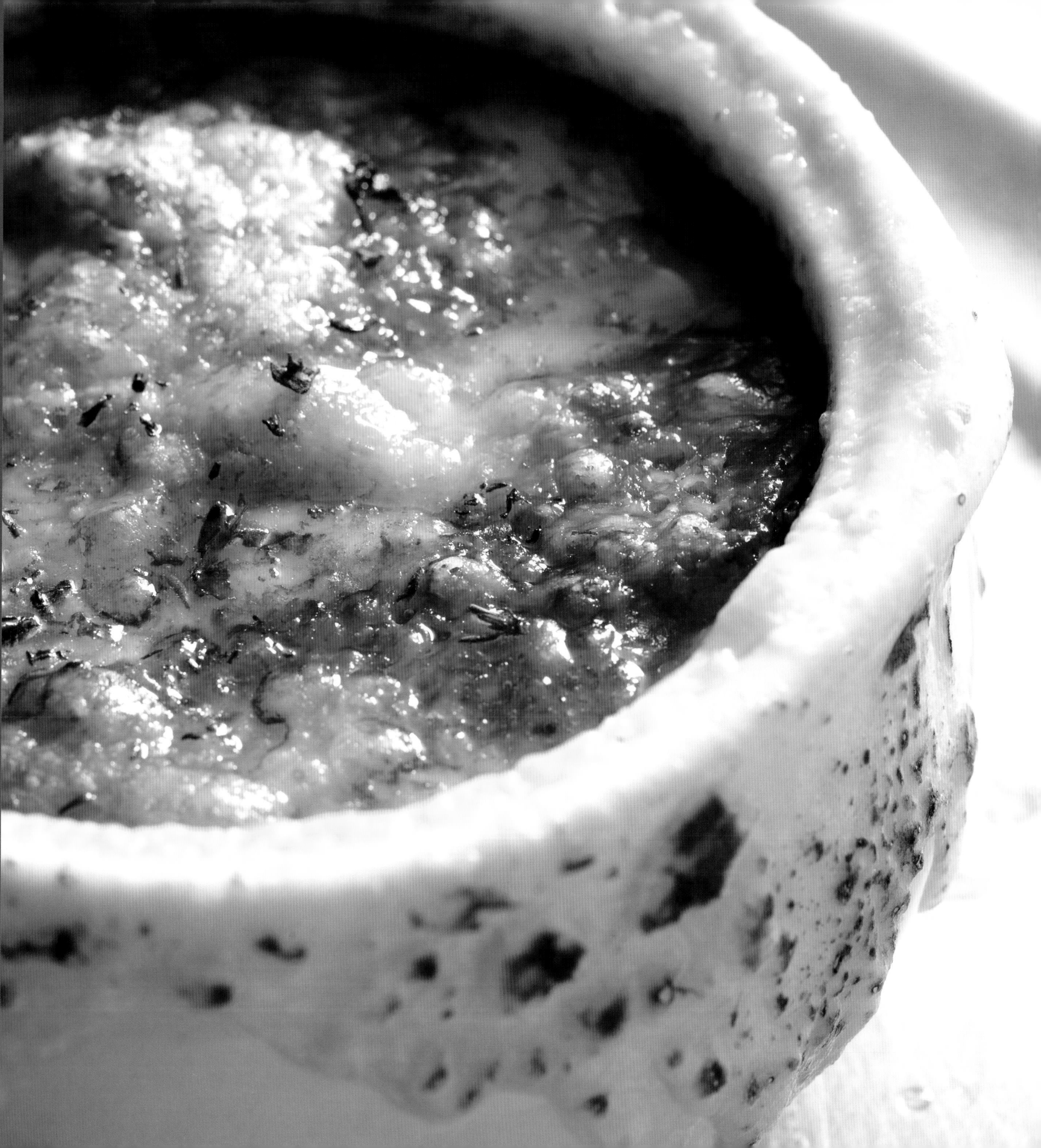

1 tablespoon vegetable oil
1 tablespoon unsalted butter
4 large onions, sliced
1 stalk celery, finely chopped
1 leek, finely chopped
½ teaspoon salt
¼ teaspoon pepper
½ cup all-purpose flour
1 cup red wine
1 cup Port wine
1 tablespoon brown sugar
1 bay leaf
½ teaspoon minced garlic
2 quarts beef broth
1 sprig thyme
1 sprig rosemary
1 sprig sage
8 French baguette slices, ¼ inch thick
4 thin slices Gruyère cheese
½ teaspoon chopped fresh thyme

Onion Soup Gratinée

Serves 4

You can't be a French chef—or in Jani's case, ever train in French cuisine—without learning to turn out one of the culture's true international classics. This soup is awesome all by itself, savory from the beef broth but also sweet from the caramelized onions. The Gruyère melted atop the baguette slices makes the whole thing way too good.

In a large stock pot, heat the oil and butter and briefly sauté onions, celery and leek with salt and pepper. Onions should to taste sweet, not bitter from getting burned. Sift the flour on top of the vegetables, stirring to break up any lumps. Add the red wine and Port along with the brown sugar, letting the liquid reduce by half. Add bay leaf, garlic, broth and aromatic herbs. Simmer over low heat for an hour to an hour and a half.

To serve, preheat oven to broil. Pour soup into individual ovenproof bowls. Cover each with two baguette slices. Put two Gruyère slices on each bowl. Set under the broiler and "gratinée" until the cheese is bubbly and golden brown. Remove from the oven and sprinkle with the chopped fresh thyme.

CORN BREAD:

1 tablespoon unsalted butter

1 cup corn flour

1 cup plus 1 tablespoon all-purpose flour

1 cup sugar

¼ tablespoon baking powder

½ teaspoon salt

4 egg whites

1 cup whole milk

Zest of 1 lemon

1 stick unsalted butter, melted

TRES LECHES MIXTURE:

2 cups heavy cream

1 cup milk

1 cup condensed milk

⅔ cup sugar

1 teaspoon vanilla extract

VANILLA PANNA COTTA:

3 cups heavy cream

1 cup milk

⅔ cup sugar

1 teaspoon vanilla extract

2 tablespoons plus 2 teaspoons
  powdered gelatin

RASPBERRY SORBET:

½ cup sugar

½ cup water

1 cup raspberries

2 tablespoons lemon juice

RASPBERRY COULIS:

3 cups fresh raspberries

½ cup sugar

1 cup water

1 tablespoon lemon juice

Vanilla Panna Cotta with Tres Leches Corn Bread, Raspberry Sorbet and Raspberry Coulis

Serves 8

For the longest time, panna cotta and tres leches seemed to be doing just fine as separate desserts—the first appearing almost exclusively in Italian restaurants, the second almost exclusively in Mexican and Central American restaurants. Leave it to a French chef and a Finnish chef to decide they belong on the same plate!

To make the corn bread, preheat the oven to 300° F. Brush a corn bread mold with the 1 tablespoon of butter and coat with flour. Mix corn flour, all-purpose flour, sugar, baking powder and salt in a large bowl. In another bowl, mix egg whites, milk, lemon zest and melted butter. Incorporate wet ingredients into the dry ingredients. Pour the mixture into prepared mold and bake for 15 to 20 minutes.

Remove the corn bread from the oven and let cool. Mix the tres leches ingredients together and soak corn bread in the mixture overnight.

To make the panna cotta, warm the milk and cream together over low heat. Meanwhile, mix the sugar and vanilla in a large bowl. Stir the warm liquid into the sugar, then stir in the gelatin. Pour the liquid into panna cotta molds and place in the refrigerator for a minimum of 3 hours.

To make the sorbet, make a simple syrup by bringing sugar and water to a boil, then let cool. Put all the ingredients in a blender, blending until smooth. Strain raspberry sauce through a sieve to remove seeds. Put in an ice cream machine, following product instructions to make a sorbet. Keep frozen.

To make the raspberry coulis, cook all ingredients over low heat for about 10 to 15 minutes. Place mixture in a blender until smooth and pass through a fine sieve.

To assemble the dessert, place panna cotta on dessert plates with the tres leches corn bread and a side of raspberry sorbet. Top with the raspberry coulis.

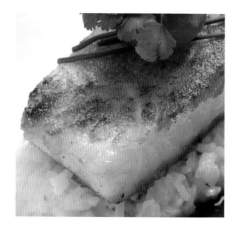

Chicken Stock

5   pounds chicken wings

1   tablespoon extra-virgin olive oil

1   leek, roughly chopped

1   bunch Italian parsley

1   bay leaf

1   large onion, chopped

1   large carrot

2½ gallons water

Preheat the oven to 400° F.

Roast chicken wings for about 25 minutes until golden.

Meanwhile heat olive oil in a large saucepan over high heat and sauté leek, parsley, bay leaf, onion and carrot. Put chicken and vegetables in a stock pot over medium-high heat. Add water, bring to a boil and simmer for 4 hours.

Pass stock through a fine sieve.

Duck Stock

5   pounds duck bones

2   carrots, chopped

1   onion, chopped

3   cloves garlic

½   cup vegetable oil

1   gallon plus 1 quart water

1   bay leaf

1   sprig fresh thyme

2   cups white wine

Preheat the oven to 375° F.

Put duck bones on a sheet pan and roast until dark brown, about 45 minutes.

Meanwhile, in a large stock pot over medium heat, sauté carrots, onion and garlic in oil until light brown. Remove bones from the oven and add them to the sautéed vegetables. Cover everything with water, and add bay leaf, thyme and white wine. Slowly simmer for 2 hours.

Pass stock through a fine sieve.

Crawfish Stock

5   pounds live crawfish

¼   cup vegetable oil

½   cup pastis

1   head fennel, chopped

1   stalk celery, chopped

1   onion, chopped

2   cups white wine

1   gallon plus 1 quart water

2   tablespoons tomato paste

Cook crawfish in oil until the crawfish turn red. Flambé crawfish with pastis.

Add fennel, celery stick and onion, and cook together over low heat for 15 minutes. Add the rest of the ingredients. Simmer for 2 hours.

Blend everything together in a food processor and pass through a fine sieve.

Lamb Stock

10 pounds lamb bones

2   carrots, chopped

2   onions, chopped

4   shallots, chopped

1   head unpeeled garlic

1   tablespoon extra-virgin olive oil

2   bay leaves

1   sprig fresh thyme

2   sprigs fresh rosemary

5   gallons plus 1 quart water

1   bottle white wine

Preheat the oven to 375° F.

Spread the bones on a large sheet pan and roast until they are browned, about 1 hour.

Meanwhile, in a large stock pot, lightly caramelize carrots, onions, shallots and garlic head in olive oil. Put roasted bones on top of the sautéed vegetables. Add bay leaves, thyme, rosemary, water and wine. Simmer over low heat for 2 to 3 hours.

Pass stock through a fine sieve.

Veal Stock

10 pounds veal bones

3 carrots, chopped

3 unpeeled onions, chopped

1 stalk celery, chopped

1 head unpeeled garlic, chopped

1 tablespoon extra-virgin olive oil

2 bay leaves

5 sprigs fresh thyme

5 gallons plus 1 quart water

2 (12-ounce) cans tomato paste

Preheat the oven to 375° F.

Spread bones on a large sheet pan and roast until browned, about 1 hour.

Meanwhile, in a large stock pot over medium heat, lightly caramelize carrots, onions, celery and garlic in olive oil. Place roasted bones on top of the sautéed vegetables. Add bay leaves, thyme and water.

Spoon tomato paste into a sauté pan and stir over medium-low heat until it's a deep reddish-brown. Incorporate into stock. Simmer over low heat for 5 to 6 hours.

Pass stock through a fine sieve.

Veal Demi–Glace

Prepare veal stock (see above), then reduce for 6 additional hours. Demi-glace will be dark, intense and syrupy.

Tomato Coulis

½ cup extra-virgin olive oil

3 carrots, peeled and finely chopped

3 onions, peeled and finely chopped

30 Roma tomatoes, peeled

1 tablespoon minced garlic

7 leaves fresh basil, chopped

Salt and pepper

Pour olive oil in a large stock pot and lightly brown the carrots and onions until light brown. Add tomatoes and garlic, and cook for 3 and a half hours over low heat. Add chopped fresh basil and continue cooking for another 30 minutes. Salt and pepper to taste.

Light Roux

1   pound unsalted butter

1   pound all-purpose flour

Preheat the oven to 375° F.

Melt butter in a pot. Slowly incorporate the flour over medium-low heat, stirring with a wooden spoon. Put the pot in the oven, stirring every 10 minutes.

Light brown roux will take 10 minutes. A darker roux will take 15 to 20 minutes.

Balsamic Reduction

1   cup veal stock *(see recipe p. 186)*

1   cup balsamic vinegar

½   cup port wine

½   cup water

1   tablespoon butter

Combine all ingredients except butter in a saucepan. Let the mixture reduce over low heat until it reaches a syrupy consistency, about 30 minutes. Remove from the heat and stir in the butter.

Basil Pesto

1   teaspoon salt

3   pounds fresh basil

1   bunch Italian parsley

1   cup extra-virgin olive oil

Salt and pepper

Bring a large pot of water with salt to a boil. Add basil leaves and Italian parsley, then quickly plunge in a bowl of ice water. Transfer from the ice water to a blender with the olive oil. Blend until smooth. Salt and pepper to taste.

Note: This is not a basil pesto for pasta; it is for decoration purposes only.

A Chef's Guide to Fresh Herbs

Chefs David and Jani love fresh herbs. In fact, most days of the year, you'll find few to no dried herbs in their kitchens. The flavors are that much better, and the availability has come a long way in recent years. More everyday grocery stores have a decent selection, plus there are more and better resources for people who want to grow their own. Here's a quick overview of some of David's and Jani's favorites.

Catnip

A member of the mint family, catnip is best known today for producing a pleasant euphoria in felines who take a "nip." But it has been a familiar herb in European kitchen gardens as far back as the thirteenth century. The leaves can be chopped and sprinkled into green salads. You can add fresh or dried leaves to soups, stews and hearty sauces.

Cilantro

Once largely unknown in the United States, the tender-stemmed green leaves that many mistake for parsley are staples of several wildly popular cuisines—from Mexican and Tex-Mex to Vietnamese, Thai and Indian. Actually a member of the carrot family, cilantro is sometimes called Chinese parsley or coriander leaves.

Golden Lemon Thyme

This is a variegated form of lemon thyme that sports golden-edged leaves. It is colorful and surprisingly fragrant of lemons. The variegation is less pronounced during the hot, sunny days of summer. This fragrant herb is particularly good for fish and chicken.

Golden Sage

In terms of flavor, this herb can be substituted in any recipe calling for generic sage. Its fresh leaves make a lovely garnish for roasted chicken or turkey. Like most garden sages, it is a short-lived perennial and needs to be replaced every second or third year.

Gorizia Rosemary

This is a unique version of rosemary with long, broad leaves that reach out from thick, rigidly upright stems. The leaves are fat and long, double the size of more ordinary varieties. The aroma of the leaves is not overpowering; it is considered gentle, sweet, perhaps a bit gingery.

Lemon Balm

Not to be confused with "bee balm" (despite the word "Melissa" in its official name, Greek for "honey bee"), this is a perennial herb of the mint family Lamiaceae that's native to southern Europe and the entire Mediterranean region. The leaves have a gentle lemon scent.

Lemon Thyme

This may look like English thyme and grow like English thyme, but the similarity ends as soon as you start to sniff and taste. The herb definitely smells and tastes like lemon, making it just the thing in any recipe calling for lemon juice or lemon zest. It is especially good in marinades.

Lime Thyme

Despite the delightful rhyme that causes people to just smile when they say it, lime thyme might be referred to as Lemon Thyme Light. It features a hint of the citrusy scent and taste that marks its more pronounced sibling, perfect for those recipes where you simply want the herb taste with less of the lemon.

Provençal Lavender

Native to the Mediterranean regions of Europe and south to Africa, lavender is first and foremost a beautiful color that covers the hillsides of Provence. In recent years, it has come into its own as a culinary herb. Long an element of the mix sold as herbes de Provence, lavender needs to be an accent, not the main flavor in a dish.

Spearmint

This is a species of mint native to much of Europe and southwest Asia, though its exact natural range is unclear thanks to extensive early cultivation. Its pointed leaf tip explain the use of the word "spear." In addition to both savory and sweet dishes, spearmint is an ingredient in several mixed drinks, including the mojito and the mint julep.

Spicy Oregano

In a culture that loves "hot and spicy" almost anything, it's about time somebody came up with this extra-pungent version of oregano. It tastes like typical oregano except more so, making it perfect for Provençal dishes as well as favorites from Italy and Greece. A significant portion of today's commercial crop comes from Israel.

Sweet Marjoram

This herb is now a naturalized citizen of southern Europe, though it once was limited to North Africa and Southeast Asia. The Greeks called this plant "joy of the mountain." Sweet marjoram is always part of a classic bouquet garni, used to flavor soups, stews and sauces.

Tricolor Sage

A member of the mint family that's attractive to bees, butterflies and chefs, this one's a cultivar of the typical culinary sage so familiar from recipes. It's actually most popular for its decorative qualities—marbled with grayish-green, white and purple, and then edged with pink. The leaves are strongly aromatic, whether used fresh or dry.

Tuscan Blue Rosemary

Here's an elegant spin on the typical rosemary, taking its name for the dark blue flowers that bloom among the reddish-brown stems with glossy green leaves. It is excellent for use in cooking, though its flavor can be intense. It's best to use it sparingly.

Winter Savory

Another favorite from southern Europe, winter savory has a reputation for going very well with both beans and meats, especially the lighter meats like chicken and turkey. It is particularly wonderful in stuffing for these and other birds. The flavor is strong when uncooked but mellows out nicely during cooking.

En premier, thanks to my wife, Elena, who truly understands friendship, love and joie de vivre and has helped me follow my destiny. Emily and Luc, my children, just looking at you smiling everyday gives me so much energy and inspiration.

This book could not have come about without the help and inspiration of many individuals: Sylvia, Gilles and Estelle Martinez, Frederique and Pascale Cercio and many others. A big thank-you for all the support from the oil companies from the Energy Corridor of Houston, Texas. And I could never leave out my thanks to all my customers at Le Mistral Restaurant for their support and their patronage.

Thank you to my friend and mentor Emmanuel Steffgen, a very important chef in my culinary life. For all those years of sharing millions and millions of recipes with me, I love you, "Manu." I would certainly like to thank all our staff of Le Mistral Restaurant who gives us constructive input. A special thank-you to Florence Lévêque for all her extra time, effort and support, typing all these recipes.

Also, thank you to my "second brother," Chef Jani Lehtinen, for all the fun we had creating this cookbook together; thanks to his lovely family and all his staff at Bucco Restaurant in Pori for the warm welcome in Finland. John DeMers, I don't know how you translate my French into readable English, but you did it. Shannon O'Hara, even a black rock on the middle of a plate would look good coming from your camera. You guys are both very talented and very patient. I am ready to go on new adventures with you anytime.

Last, but not least, I want to thank my brother, Sylvain Denis, for all these years working together, for better and for worse, to put the restaurant where it is. And a big thank-you to Mémé Garnero and Maman Denis, who live so far away from me but are always part of my heart.

– DAVID DENIS

First I want to thank my wife, Sani, for all the support that she has given me through the years, for helping me to become a better chef every day, for reminding me to keep my feet on the ground, even when my head is high in the sky. Warm hugs to our three children—Anna, Eemeli and Aino—for being an overwhelming inspiration for me, as well as for being challenging food critics on a daily basis.

I want to thank Chef Svein and Anne-Torill, Chef Erling and Gunn Elis for making my trips to Houston a reality in the first place; also special thanks to Svein for taking me to dinner at Le Mistral on my first night in Houston. That is how I first met David and Sylvain. Big thanks to Tommi Matomäki, Rolf Öhman, Sinikka Uusitalo at Technip Pori, David Dickson, Steve Allen and Alice and Marci at Technip Houston. Thanks and kisses to Don and Ann Vardeman and all the great friends and people at Anadarko Petroleum Company. From Shell, I want to thank Curtis "Bam" Lohr, Paul and Michelle Dixon, Walter "Wally" Shannon and all the rest. From Chevron, Gary Luquette for good company during all the Finnish dinners and almost at the golf course (too much rain).

Special thanks to Per and Misusu for teaching me how to make perfect Japanese cuisine, and to Torske Runk. *Kaunis kiitos* to my gastronomic brother, Chef Jari Seppälä in Bucco´s kitchen, as well Päivi, Janne, Juha, Heli, Carita and Katri, without whom Bucco would not be the great restaurant it is today.

Thanks to my dear friends and mentors, Hans Välimäki, Jarkko Erkkilä and Mika Kansanniva.

Thanks to Juuti and Hanna for a great friendship and all the colorful dinner experiences (and wines) during the past two decades; I hope for another 50 years to come.

Grazie mille to Maestro Ilkka Haaslahti for good friendship and hunting all that wild game so we can prepare such great food. Also thank you for heating the sauna. *Merci beaucoup* to the big and warm-hearted family of David in Provence; we are coming back for sure.

Big thanks to Osuusmeijeri Satamaito and Jarmo Oksman for presenting a perfect place to make Bucco. I want to thank the city of Pori and all the wonderful and hungry customers of Bucco for so many great memories.

I want to thank Sylvain and Katie and all the staff at Le Mistral for making me feel at home more and more with every visit. And also Elena, Emilie and Luc for nice family moments at your home. And last Chef David, my friend. After all this fun, I feel like I'm married to you—gastronomically of course. Let's make another cookbook! John, Shannon! Come on boys, let's go.

– JANI LEHTINEN

Our Staffs

INDEX

INDEX

JOHN DEMERS

A native of New Orleans, with parents who loved to cook together and discuss recipes while drinking cans of Dixie beer, John DeMers spent many years in the news business covering all the usual Mafia trials and plane crashes. He later ate his way through 136 foreign countries before realizing he could get pretty much the same food somewhere in Texas. He has served as food editor of the wire service United Press International, as well as of the *Houston Chronicle*. For more than 20 years, John has hosted the Delicious Mischief radio show, first in his hometown and now in Houston on NewsRadio 740 KTRH and in Austin on Talk 1370. He is the author of 40 books, the first 39 of which were nonfiction about food, wine and travel. His latest, *Marfa Shadows,* marks his entry into the mystery fiction field, launching a series that, of course, had to be set in and around a restaurant and star a Texas chef. John's second great love has always been the arts, covering things like opera, ballet and theater and serving for several years as editor of *ArtsHouston* magazine. This interest eventually led him to create two musicals of his own, *Deep in the Heart* (which debuted at the Hobby Center for the Performing Arts before touring Texas) and *Texas at Heart.* John is the father of four mostly grown children, and he often finds himself more fascinated by what they're doing than what he's doing.

Shannon O'Hara grew up on the campus of Tougaloo College in Tougaloo, Mississippi, where his father is an art professor while his mother teaches art at the Mississippi School of the Arts. A chronic daydreamer, Shannon left home at 16 to pursue his dream of becoming a professional ballet dancer, a fascination that eventually earned him a job as a dancer with the Houston Ballet, the nation's fourth largest company. A similar fascination later carried him to New York, where he spent 10 years working and studying photography at the International Center of Photography and The School of Visual Arts. He furthered his professional education with food photography work on cookbooks at the Culinary Institute of America in Hyde Park, as well as by assisting some of the top New York photographers, including legendary Magnum master Bruce Davidson and renowned food and travel photographer Ben Fink. Shannon has returned to Houston to explore the life and culture that he left so long ago. His work has been published in *Food and Wine, Gourmet, Esquire, Texas Monthly, Wine Spectator, Houston Modern Luxury, Dallas Modern Luxury, Go, Forbes Traveler* and *Market Watch* magazines. Shannon met his wife, Evelin, while both were attending the High School for Performing and Visual Arts in Houston. She is a senior art director with Digital DraftFCB in New York and specializes in graphic animation. They have a five-year-old daughter named Leila who, not at all surprisingly, really loves to draw.

Conversion Tables

WEIGHTS		
US		Metric
½ oz	=	15g
1 oz	=	25g
1 ½ oz	=	40g
2 oz	=	50g
3 oz	=	75g
4 oz	=	100g
5 oz	=	150g
6 oz	=	175g
7 oz	=	200g
8 oz	=	225g
9 oz	=	250g
10 oz	=	275g
12 oz	=	350g
13 oz	=	375g
14 oz	=	400g
15 oz	=	425g
1 lb	=	450g

VOLUME		
US		Metric
1 tsp	=	5 ml
1 tbsp	=	15 ml
1 fl oz	=	29 ml
2 fl oz	=	58 ml
3 fl oz	=	87 ml
½ cup	=	125 ml
2/3 cup	=	148 ml
¾ cup	=	177 ml
1 cup	=	250 ml
1 pint	=	600 ml
1 quart	=	945 ml
1 gallon	=	3.75 liters

TEMPERATURES	
F	C
275	140
300	150
325	160
350	180
375	190
400	200
425	220
450	230
475	240